110TH CONGRESS 1st Session } HOUSE OF REPRESENTATIVES { DOCUMENT No. 110–50

THE CONSTITUTION OF THE UNITED STATES OF AMERICA

As Amended

Unratified Amendments

Analytical Index

PRESENTED BY MR. BRADY
OF PENNSYLVANIA

July 25, 2007 • Ordered to be printed

UNITED STATES
GOVERNMENT PRINTING OFFICE
WASHINGTON: 2007

For sale by the Superintendent of Documents, U.S. Government Printing Office
Internet: bookstore.gpo.gov Phone: toll free (866) 512-1800; DC area (202) 512-1800
Fax: (202) 512-2104 Mail: Stop IDCC, Washington, DC 20402-001
[ISBN 978–0–16–079091–1]

House Doc. 110–50

The printing of the revised version of The Constitution of the United States of America As Amended (Document Size) is hereby ordered pursuant to H. Con. Res. 190 as passed on July 25, 2007, 110th Congress, 1st Session. This document was compiled at the direction of Chairman Robert A. Brady of the Joint Committee on Printing, and printed by the U.S. Government Printing Office.

CONTENTS

Historical Note v
Text of the Constitution 1
Amendments 13
Proposed Amendments Not Ratified 29
Index to the Constitution and Amendments 33

"Scene at the Signing of the Constitution of the United States"

By Howard Chandler Christy.
Provided by the Architect of the Capitol.

HISTORICAL NOTE

The Delegates who convened at the Federal Convention on May 25, 1787, quickly rejected the idea of revising the Articles of Confederation and agreed to construct a new framework for a national government. Throughout the summer months at the Convention in Philadelphia, delegates from 12 States debated the proper form such a government should take, but few questioned the need to establish a more vigorous government to preside over the union of States. The 39 delegates who signed the Constitution on September 17, 1787, expected the new charter to provide a permanent guarantee of the political liberties achieved in the Revolution.

Prior to the adoption of the Federal Constitution, an Articles of Confederation, drafted by the Continental Congress and approved by 13 States, provided for a union of the former British colonies. Even before Maryland became the last State to accede to the Articles in 1781, a number of Americans, particularly those involved in the prosecution of the Revolutionary War, recognized the inadequacies of the Articles as a national government. In the 1780s these nationally-minded Americans became increasingly disturbed by the Articles' failure to provide the central government with authority to raise revenue, regulate commerce, or enforce treaties.

Despite repeated proposals that the Continental Congress revise the Articles, the movement for a new national government began outside the Congress. Representatives of Maryland and Virginia, meeting at Mt. Vernon to discuss trade problems between the two States, agreed to invite delegates from all States to discuss commercial affairs at a meeting in Annapolis, Maryland, in September 1786. Although delegates from only five States reached the Annapolis Convention, that group issued a call for a meeting of all States to discuss necessary revisions of the Articles of Confederation. Responding to this call and the endorsement of the Continental Congress, every State except Rhode Island selected delegates for the meeting in the State House at Philadelphia.

The document printed here was the product of nearly 4 months of deliberations in the Federal Convention at Philadelphia. The challenging task before the delegates was to create a republican form of government that could encompass the 13 States and accommodate the anticipated expansion to the West. The distribution of authority between legislative, executive, and judicial branches was a boldly original attempt to create an energetic central government at the same time that the sovereignty of the people was preserved.

The longest debate of the Convention centered on the proper form of representation and election for the Congress. The division between small States that wished to perpetuate the equal representation of States in the Continental Congress and the large States that proposed representation proportional to population threatened to bring the Convention proceedings to a halt. Over several weeks the delegates developed a complicated compromise that provided for equal representation of the States in a Senate elected by State legislature and proportional representation in a popularly-elected House of Representatives.

The conflict between large and small States disappeared in the early years of the republic. More lasting was the division between slave and free States that had been a disturbing undercurrent in the Convention debates. The Convention's strained attempt to avoid using the word slavery in the articles granting recognition and protection to that institution scarcely hid the regional divisions that would remain unresolved under the terms of union agreed to in 1787.

The debates in the State ratification conventions of 1787 and 1788 made clear the need to provide amendments to the basic framework drafted in Philadelphia. Beginning with Massachusetts, a number of State conventions ratified the Constitution with the request that a bill of rights be added to protect certain liberties at the core of English and American political traditions. The First Congress approved a set of amendments which became the Bill of Rights when ratified by the States in 1791. The continuing process of amendment, clearly described in the note of the following text, has enabled the Constitution to accommodate changing conditions in American society at the same time that the Founders' basic outline of national government remains intact.

CONSTITUTION OF THE UNITED STATES [1]

WE THE PEOPLE of the United States, in Order to form a more perfect Union, establish Justice, insure domestic Tranquility, provide for the common defence, promote the general Welfare, and secure the Blessings of Liberty to ourselves and our Posterity, do ordain and establish this Constitution for the United States of America.

ARTICLE I.

SECTION 1. All legislative Powers herein granted shall be vested in a Congress of the United States, which shall consist of a Senate and House of Representatives.

---

[1] This text of the Constitution follows the engrossed copy signed by Gen. Washington and the deputies from 12 States. The small superior figures preceding the paragraphs designate clauses, and were not in the original and have no reference to footnotes.

The Constitution was adopted by a convention of the States on September 17, 1787, and was subsequently ratified by the several States, on the following dates: Delaware, December 7, 1787; Pennsylvania, December 12, 1787; New Jersey, December 18, 1787; Georgia, January 2, 1788; Connecticut, January 9, 1788; Massachusetts, February 6, 1788; Maryland, April 28, 1788; South Carolina, May 23, 1788; New Hampshire, June 21, 1788.

Ratification was completed on June 21, 1788.

The Constitution was subsequently ratified by Virginia, June 25, 1788; New York, July 26, 1788; North Carolina, November 21, 1789; Rhode Island, May 29, 1790; and Vermont, January 10, 1791.

In May 1785, a committee of Congress made a report recommending an alteration in the Articles of Confederation, but no action was taken on it, and it was left to the State Legislatures to proceed in the matter. In January 1786, the Legislature of Virginia passed a resolution providing for the appointment of five commissioners, who, or any three of them, should meet such commissioners as might be appointed in the other States of the Union, at a time and place to be agreed upon, to take into consideration the trade of the United States; to consider how far a uniform system in their commercial regulations may be necessary to their common interest and their permanent harmony; and to report to the several States such an act, relative to this great object, as, when ratified by them, will enable the United States in Congress effectually to provide for the same. The Virginia commissioners, after some correspondence, fixed the first Monday in September as the time, and the city of Annapolis as the place for the meeting, but only four other States were represented, viz: Delaware, New York, New Jersey, and Pennsylvania; the commissioners appointed by Massachusetts, New Hampshire, North Carolina, and Rhode Island failed to attend. Under the circumstances of so partial a representation, the commissioners present agreed upon a report (drawn by Mr. Hamilton, of New York) expressing their unanimous conviction that it might essentially tend to advance the interests of the Union if the States by which they were respectively delegated would concur, and use their endeavors to procure the concurrence of the other States, in the appointment of commissioners to meet at Philadelphia on the second Monday of May following, to take into consideration the situation of the United States; to devise such further provisions as should appear to them necessary to render the Constitution of the Federal Government adequate to the exigencies of the Union; and to report such an act for that purpose to the United States in Congress assembled as, when agreed to by them and afterwards confirmed by the Legislatures of every State, would effectually provide for the same.

Congress, on the 21st of February, 1787, adopted a resolution in favor of a convention, and the Legislatures of those States which had not already done so (with the exception of Rhode Island) promptly appointed delegates. On the 25th of May, seven States having convened, George Washington, of Virginia, was unanimously elected President, and the consideration of the proposed constitution was commenced. On the 17th of September, 1787, the Constitution as engrossed and agreed upon was signed by all the members present, except Mr. Gerry of Massachusetts, and Messrs. Mason and Randolph, of Virginia. The president of the convention transmitted it to Congress, with a resolution stating how the proposed Federal Government should

Continued

SECTION 2. [1]The House of Representatives shall be composed of Members chosen every second Year by the People of the several States, and the Electors in each State shall have the Qualifications requisite for Electors of the most numerous Branch of the State Legislature.

[2]No Person shall be a Representative who shall not have attained to the Age of twenty five Years, and been seven Years a Citizen of the United States, and who shall not, when elected, be an Inhabitant of that State in which he shall be chosen.

[3]Representatives and direct Taxes shall be apportioned among the several States which may be included within this Union, according to their respective Numbers, which shall be determined by adding to the whole Number of free Persons, including those bound to Service for a Term of Years, and excluding Indians not taxed, three fifths of all other Persons.[2] The actual Enumeration shall be made within three Years after the first Meeting of the Congress of the United States, and within every subsequent Term of ten Years, in such Manner as they shall by Law direct. The Number of Representatives shall not exceed one for every thirty Thousand, but each State shall have at Least one Representative; and until such enumeration shall be made, the State of New Hampshire shall be entitled to chuse three, Massachusetts eight, Rhode Island and Providence Plantations one, Connecticut five, New York six, New Jersey four, Pennsylvania eight, Delaware one, Maryland six, Virginia ten, North Carolina five, South Carolina five, and Georgia three.

[4]When vacancies happen in the Representation from any State, the Executive Authority thereof shall issue Writs of Election to fill such Vacancies.

[5]The House of Representatives shall chuse their Speaker and other Officers; and shall have the sole Power of Impeachment.

SECTION 3. [1]The Senate of the United States shall be composed of two Senators from each State, chosen by the Legislature thereof[3] for six Years; and each Senator shall have one Vote.

[2]Immediately after they shall be assembled in Consequence of the first Election, they shall be divided as equally as may be into three Classes. The Seats of the Senators of the first Class shall be vacated at the Expiration of the second Year, of the second Class at the Expiration of the fourth Year, and of the third Class at the Expiration of the sixth Year, so that one third may be chosen every

---

be put in operation, and an explanatory letter. Congress, on the 28th of September, 1787, directed the Constitution so framed, with the resolutions and letter concerning the same, to "be transmitted to the several Legislatures in order to be submitted to a convention of delegates chosen in each State by the people thereof, in conformity to the resolves of the convention."

On the 4th of March, 1789, the day which had been fixed for commencing the operations of Government under the new Constitution, it had been ratified by the conventions chosen in each State to consider it, as follows: Delaware, December 7, 1787; Pennsylvania, December 12, 1787; New Jersey, December 18, 1787; Georgia, January 2, 1788; Connecticut, January 9, 1788; Massachusetts, February 6, 1788; Maryland, April 28, 1788; South Carolina, May 23, 1788; New Hampshire, June 21, 1788; Virginia, June 25, 1788; and New York, July 26, 1788.

The President informed Congress, on the 28th of January, 1790, that North Carolina had ratified the Constitution November 21, 1789; and he informed Congress on the 1st of June, 1790, that Rhode Island had ratified the Constitution May 29, 1790. Vermont, in convention, ratified the Constitution January 10, 1791, and was, by an act of Congress approved February 18, 1791, "received and admitted into this Union as a new and entire member of the United States."

[2]The part of this clause relating to the mode of apportionment of representatives among the several States has been affected by section 2 of amendment XIV, and as to taxes on incomes without apportionment by amendment XVI.

[3]This clause has been affected by clause 1 of amendment XVII.

second Year; and if Vacancies happen by Resignation or otherwise, during the Recess of the Legislature of any State, the Executive thereof may make temporary Appointments until the next Meeting of the Legislature, which shall then fill such Vacancies.[4]

3 No Person shall be a Senator who shall not have attained to the Age of thirty Years, and been nine Years a Citizen of the United States, and who shall not, when elected, be an Inhabitant of that State for which he shall be chosen.

4 The Vice President of the United States shall be President of the Senate, but shall have no Vote, unless they be equally divided.

5 The Senate shall chuse their other Officers, and also a President pro tempore, in the Absence of the Vice President, or when he shall exercise the Office of President of the United States.

6 The Senate shall have the sole Power to try all Impeachments. When sitting for that Purpose, they shall be on Oath or Affirmation. When the President of the United States is tried, the Chief Justice shall preside: And no Person shall be convicted without the Concurrence of two thirds of the Members present.

7 Judgment in Cases of Impeachment shall not extend further than to removal from Office, and disqualification to hold and enjoy any Office of honor, Trust or Profit under the United States: but the Party convicted shall nevertheless be liable and subject to Indictment, Trial, Judgment and Punishment, according to Law.

SECTION 4. 1 The Times, Places and Manner of holding Elections for Senators and Representatives, shall be prescribed in each State by the Legislature thereof; but the Congress may at any time by Law make or alter such Regulations, except as to the Places of chusing Senators.

2 The Congress shall assemble at least once in every Year and such Meeting shall be on the first Monday in December,[5] unless they shall by Law appoint a different Day.

SECTION 5. 1 Each House shall be the Judge of the Elections, Returns and Qualifications of its own Members, and a Majority of each shall constitute a Quorum to do Business; but a smaller Number may adjourn from day to day, and may be authorized to compel the Attendance of absent Members, in such Manner, and under such Penalties as each House may provide.

2 Each House may determine the Rules of its Proceedings, punish its Members for disorderly Behavior, and, with the Concurrence of two thirds, expel a Member.

3 Each House shall keep a Journal of its Proceedings, and from time to time publish the same, excepting such Parts as may in their Judgment require Secrecy; and the Yeas and Nays of the Members of either House on any question shall, at the Desire of one fifth of those Present, be entered on the Journal.

4 Neither House, during the Session of Congress, shall, without the Consent of the other, adjourn for more than three days, nor to any other Place than that in which the two Houses shall be sitting.

SECTION 6. 1 The Senators and Representatives shall receive a Compensation for their Services, to be ascertained by Law, and

---

[4] This clause has been affected by clause 2 of amendment XVIII.
[5] This clause has been affected by amendment XX.

paid out of the Treasury of the United States.[6] They shall in all Cases, except Treason, Felony and Breach of the Peace, be privileged from Arrest during their Attendance at the Session of their respective Houses, and in going to and returning from the same; and for any Speech or Debate in either House, they shall not be questioned in any other Place.

[2] No Senator or Representative shall, during the Time for which he was elected, be appointed to any civil Office under the Authority of the United States, which shall have been created, or the Emoluments whereof shall have been encreased during such time; and no Person holding any Office under the United States, shall be a Member of either House during his Continuance in Office.

SECTION 7. [1] All Bills for raising Revenue shall originate in the House of Representatives; but the Senate may propose or concur with Amendments as on other Bills.

[2] Every Bill which shall have passed the House of Representatives and the Senate, shall, before it become a Law, be presented to the President of the United States; If he approve he shall sign it, but if not he shall return it, with his Objections to that House in which it shall have originated, who shall enter the Objections at large on their Journal, and proceed to reconsider it. If after such Reconsideration two thirds of that House shall agree to pass the Bill, it shall be sent, together with the Objections, to the other House, by which it shall likewise be reconsidered, and if approved by two thirds of that House, it shall become a Law. But in all such Cases the Votes of both Houses shall be determined by Yeas and Nays, and the Names of the Persons voting for and against the Bill shall be entered on the Journal of each House respectively. If any Bill shall not be returned by the President within ten Days (Sundays excepted) after it shall have been presented to him, the Same shall be a Law, in like Manner as if he had signed it, unless the Congress by their Adjournment prevent its Return, in which Case it shall not be a Law.

[3] Every Order, Resolution, or Vote to which the Concurrence of the Senate and House of Representatives may be necessary (except on a question of Adjournment) shall be presented to the President of the United States; and before the Same shall take Effect, shall be approved by him, or being disapproved by him, shall be repassed by two thirds of the Senate and House of Representatives, according to the Rules and Limitations prescribed in the Case of a Bill.

SECTION 8. [1] The Congress shall have Power To lay and collect Taxes, Duties, Imposts and Excises, to pay the Debts and provide for the common Defence and general Welfare of the United States; but all Duties, Imposts and Excises shall be uniform throughout the United States;

[2] To borrow Money on the credit of the United States;

[3] To regulate Commerce with foreign Nations, and among the several States, and with the Indian Tribes;

[4] To establish a uniform Rule of Naturalization, and uniform Laws on the subject of Bankruptcies throughout the United States;

[5] To coin Money, regulate the Value thereof, and of foreign Coin, and fix the Standard of Weights and Measures;

---

[6] This clause has been affected by amendment XXVII.

[6] To provide for the Punishment of counterfeiting the Securities and current Coin of the United States;

[7] To establish Post Offices and post Roads;

[8] To promote the Progress of Science and useful Arts, by securing for limited Times to Authors and Inventors the exclusive Right to their respective Writings and Discoveries;

[9] To constitute Tribunals inferior to the supreme Court;

[10] To define and punish Piracies and Felonies committed on the high Seas, and Offences against the Law of Nations;

[11] To declare War, grant Letters of Marque and Reprisal, and make Rules concerning Captures on Land and Water;

[12] To raise and support Armies, but no Appropriation of Money to that Use shall be for a longer Term than two Years;

[13] To provide and maintain a Navy;

[14] To make Rules for the Government and Regulation of the land and naval Forces;

[15] To provide for calling forth the Militia to execute the Laws of the Union, suppress Insurrections and repel Invasions;

[16] To provide for organizing, arming, and disciplining, the Militia, and for governing such Part of them as may be employed in the Service of the United States, reserving to the States respectively, the Appointment of the Officers, and the Authority of training the Militia according to the discipline prescribed by Congress;

[17] To exercise exclusive Legislation in all Cases whatsoever, over such District (not exceeding ten Miles square) as may, by Cession of particular States, and the Acceptance of Congress, become the Seat of the Government of the United States, and to exercise like Authority over all Places purchased by the Consent of the Legislature of the State in which the Same shall be, for the Erection of Forts, Magazines, Arsenals, dock-Yards, and other needful buildings;—And

[18] To make all Laws which shall be necessary and proper for carrying into Execution the foregoing Powers, and all other Powers vested by this Constitution in the Government of the United States, or in any Department or Officer thereof.

SECTION 9. [1] The Migration or Importation of such Persons as any of the States now existing shall think proper to admit, shall not be prohibited by the Congress prior to the Year one thousand eight hundred and eight, but a Tax or duty may be imposed on such Importation, not exceeding ten dollars for each Person.

[2] The Privilege of the Writ of Habeas Corpus shall not be suspended, unless when in Cases of Rebellion or Invasion the public Safety may require it.

[3] No Bill of Attainder or ex post facto Law shall be passed.

[4] No Capitation, or other direct, Tax shall be laid, unless in Proportion to the Census or Enumeration herein before directed to be taken.[7]

[5] No Tax or Duty shall be laid on Articles exported from any State.

[6] No Preference shall be given by any Regulation of Commerce or Revenue to the Ports of one State over those of another: nor shall

[7] This clause has been affected by amendment XVI.

Vessels bound to, or from, one State, be obliged to enter, clear, or pay Duties in another.

[7] No Money shall be drawn from the Treasury, but in Consequence of Appropriations made by Law; and a regular Statement and Account of the Receipts and Expenditures of all public Money shall be published from time to time.

[8] No Title of Nobility shall be granted by the United States: And no Person holding any Office of Profit or Trust under them, shall, without the Consent of the Congress, accept of any present, Emolument, Office, or Title, of any kind whatever, from any King, Prince, or foreign State.

SECTION 10. [1] No State shall enter into any Treaty, Alliance, or Confederation; grant Letters of Marque and Reprisal; coin Money; emit Bills of Credit; make any Thing but gold and silver Coin a Tender in Payment of Debts; pass any Bill of Attainder, ex post facto Law, or Law impairing the Obligation of Contracts, or grant any Title of Nobility.

[2] No State shall, without the Consent of the Congress, lay any Imposts or Duties on Imports or Exports, except what may be absolutely necessary for executing its inspection Laws: and the net Produce of all Duties and Imposts, laid by any State on Imports or Exports, shall be for the Use of the Treasury of the United States; and all such Laws shall be subject to the Revision and Control of the Congress.

[3] No State shall, without the Consent of Congress, lay any Duty of Tonnage, keep Troops, or Ships of War in time of Peace, enter into any Agreement or Compact with another State, or with a foreign Power, or engage in War, unless actually invaded, or in such imminent Danger as will not admit of delay.

ARTICLE II.

SECTION 1. [1] The executive Power shall be vested in a President of the United States of America. He shall hold his Office during the Term of four Years, and, together with the Vice President, chosen for the same Term, be elected, as follows

[2] Each State shall appoint, in such Manner as the Legislature thereof may direct, a Number of Electors, equal to the whole Number of Senators and Representatives to which the State may be entitled in the Congress: but no Senator or Representative, or Person holding an Office of Trust or Profit under the United States, shall be appointed an Elector.

[3] The Electors shall meet in their respective States, and vote by Ballot for two Persons, of whom one at least shall not be an Inhabitant of the same State with themselves. And they shall make a List of all the Persons voted for, and of the Number of Votes for each; which List they shall sign and certify, and transmit sealed to the Seat of the Government of the United States, directed to the President of the Senate. The President of the Senate shall, in the Presence of the Senate and House of Representatives, open all the Certificates, and the Votes shall then be counted. The Person having the greatest Number of Votes shall be the President, if such Number be a Majority of the whole Number of Electors appointed; and if there be more than one who have such Majority, and have an equal Number of Votes, then the House of Representatives shall

immediately chuse by Ballot one of them for President; and if no Person have a Majority, then from the five highest on the List the said House shall in like Manner chuse the President. But in chusing the President, the Votes shall be taken by States, the Representation from each State having one Vote; A quorum for this Purpose shall consist of a Member or Members from two thirds of the States, and a Majority of all the States shall be necessary to a Choice. In every Case, after the Choice of the President, the Person having the greatest Number of Votes of the Electors shall be the Vice President. But if there should remain two or more who have equal Votes, the Senate shall chuse from them by Ballot the Vice President.[8]

[4] The Congress may determine the Time of chusing the Electors, and the Day on which they shall give their Votes; which Day shall be the same throughout the United States.

[5] No Person except a natural born Citizen, or a Citizen of the United States, at the time of the Adoption of this Constitution, shall be eligible to the Office of President; neither shall any Person be eligible to that Office who shall not have attained to the Age of thirty five Years, and been fourteen Years a Resident within the United States.

[6] In Case of the Removal of the President from Office, or of his Death, Resignation, or Inability to discharge the Powers and Duties of the said Office,[9] the Same shall devolve on the Vice President, and the Congress may by Law provide for the Case of Removal, Death, Resignation or Inability, both of the President and Vice President, declaring what Officer shall then act as President, and such Officer shall act accordingly, until the Disability be removed, or a President shall be elected.

[7] The President shall, at stated Times, receive for his Services, a Compensation, which shall neither be encreased nor diminished during the Period for which he shall have been elected, and he shall not receive within that Period any other Emolument from the United States, or any of them.

[8] Before he enter on the Execution of his Office, he shall take the following Oath or Affirmation:—"I do solemnly swear (or affirm) that I will faithfully execute the Office of President of the United States, and will to the best of my Ability, preserve, protect and defend the Constitution of the United States."

SECTION 2. [1] The President shall be Commander in Chief of the Army and Navy of the United States, and of the Militia of the several States, when called into the actual Service of the United States; he may require the Opinion, in writing, of the principal Officer in each of the executive Departments, upon any Subject relating to the Duties of their respective Offices, and he shall have Power to grant Reprieves and Pardons for Offences against the United States, except in Cases of Impeachment.

[2] He shall have Power, by and with the Advice and Consent of the Senate, to make Treaties, provided two thirds of the Senators present concur; and he shall nominate, and by and with the Advice and Consent of the Senate, shall appoint Ambassadors, other pub-

---

[8] This clause has been superseded by amendment XII.

[9] This clause has been affected by amendment XXV.

lic Ministers and Consuls, Judges of the supreme Court, and all other Officers of the United States, whose Appointments are not herein otherwise provided for, and which shall be established by Law: but the Congress may by Law vest the Appointment of such inferior Officers, as they think proper, in the President alone, in the Courts of Law, or in the Heads of Departments.

3 The President shall have Power to fill up all Vacancies that may happen during the Recess of the Senate, by granting Commissions which shall expire at the End of their next Session.

SECTION 3. He shall from time to time give to the Congress Information of the State of the Union, and recommend to their Consideration such Measures as he shall judge necessary and expedient; he may, on extraordinary Occasions, convene both Houses, or either of them, and in Case of Disagreement between them, with Respect to the Time of Adjournment, he may adjourn them to such Time as he shall think proper; he shall receive Ambassadors and other public Ministers; he shall take Care that the Laws be faithfully executed, and shall Commission all the Officers of the United States.

SECTION 4. The President, Vice President and all civil Officers of the United States, shall be removed from Office on Impeachment for, and Conviction of, Treason, Bribery, or other high Crimes and Misdemeanors.

ARTICLE III.

SECTION 1. The judicial Power of the United States, shall be vested in one supreme Court, and in such inferior Courts as the Congress may from time to time ordain and establish. The Judges, both of the supreme and inferior Courts, shall hold their Offices during good Behaviour, and shall, at stated Times, receive for their Services, a Compensation, which shall not be diminished during their Continuance in Office.

SECTION 2. 1 The judicial Power shall extend to all Cases, in Law and Equity, arising under this Constitution, the Laws of the United States, and Treaties made, or which shall be made, under their Authority;—to all Cases affecting Ambassadors, other public Ministers and Consuls;—to all Cases of admiralty and maritime Jurisdiction;—to Controversies to which the United States will be a party;—to Controversies between two or more States;—between a State and Citizens of another State;[10]—between Citizens of different States,—between Citizens of the same State claiming Lands under Grants of different States, and between a State, or the Citizens thereof, and foreign States, Citizens or Subjects.

2 In all Cases affecting Ambassadors, other public Ministers and Consuls, and those in which a State shall be Party, the supreme Court shall have original Jurisdiction. In all the other Cases before mentioned, the supreme Court shall have appellate Jurisdiction, both as to Law and Fact, with such Exceptions, and under such Regulations as the Congress shall make.

3 The Trial of all Crimes, except in Cases of Impeachment, shall be by Jury; and such Trial shall be held in the State where the said Crimes shall have been committed; but when not committed

[10] This clause has been affected by amendment XI.

within any State, the Trial shall be at such Place or Places as the Congress may by Law have directed.

SECTION 3. [1] Treason against the United States, shall consist only in levying War against them, or in adhering to their Enemies, giving them Aid and Comfort. No Person shall be convicted of Treason unless on the Testimony of two Witnesses to the same overt Act, or on Confession in open Court.

[2] The Congress shall have Power to declare the Punishment of Treason, but no Attainder of Treason shall work Corruption of Blood, or Forfeiture except during the Life of the Person attainted.

ARTICLE IV.

SECTION 1. Full Faith and Credit shall be given in each State to the public Acts, Records, and judicial Proceedings of every other State. And the Congress may by general Laws prescribe the Manner in which such Acts, Records and Proceedings shall be proved, and the Effect thereof.

SECTION 2. [1] The Citizens of each State shall be entitled to all Privileges and Immunities of Citizens in the several States.

[2] A Person charged in any State with Treason, Felony, or other Crime, who shall flee from Justice, and be found in another State, shall on Demand of the executive Authority of the State from which he fled, be delivered up, to be removed to the State having Jurisdiction of the Crime.

[3] No Person held to Service or Labour in one State, under the Laws thereof, escaping into another, shall, in Consequence of any Law or Regulation therein, be discharged from such Service or Labour, but shall be delivered up on Claim of the Party to whom such Service or Labour may be due.[11]

SECTION 3. [1] New States may be admitted by the Congress into this Union; but no new State shall be formed or erected within the Jurisdiction of any other State; nor any State be formed by the Junction of two or more States, or Parts of States, without the Consent of the Legislatures of the States concerned as well as of the Congress.

[2] The Congress shall have Power to dispose of and make all needful Rules and Regulations respecting the Territory or other Property belonging to the United States; and nothing in this Constitution shall be so construed as to Prejudice any Claims of the United States, or of any particular State.

SECTION 4. The United States shall guarantee to every State in this Union a Republican Form of Government, and shall protect each of them against Invasion; and on Application of the Legislature, or of the Executive (when the Legislature cannot be convened) against domestic Violence.

ARTICLE V.

The Congress, whenever two thirds of both Houses shall deem it necessary, shall propose Amendments to this Constitution, or, on the Application of the Legislatures of two thirds of the several States, shall call a Convention for proposing Amendments, which,

[11] This clause has been affected by amendment XIII.

in either Case, shall be valid to all Intents and Purposes, as Part of this Constitution, when ratified by the Legislatures of three fourths of the several States, or by Conventions in three fourths thereof, as the one or the other Mode of Ratification may be proposed by the Congress; Provided that no Amendment which may be made prior to the Year One thousand eight hundred and eight shall in any Manner affect the first and fourth Clauses in the Ninth Section of the first Article; and that no State, without its Consent, shall be deprived of its equal Suffrage in the Senate.

ARTICLE VI.

1 All Debts contracted and Engagements entered into, before the Adoption of this Constitution, shall be as valid against the United States under this Constitution, as under the Confederation.

2 This Constitution, and the Laws of the United States which shall be made in Pursuance thereof; and all Treaties made, or which shall be made, under the Authority of the United States, shall be the supreme Law of the Land; and the Judges in every State shall be bound thereby, any Thing in the Constitution or Laws of any State to the Contrary notwithstanding.

3 The Senators and Representatives before mentioned, and the Members of the several State Legislatures, and all executive and judicial Officers, both of the United States and of the several States, shall be bound by Oath or Affirmation, to support this Constitution; but no religious Test shall ever be required as a Qualification to any Office or public Trust under the United States.

ARTICLE VII.

The Ratification of the Conventions of nine States, shall be sufficient for the Establishment of this Constitution between the States so ratifying the Same.

DONE in Convention by the Unanimous Consent of the States present the Seventeenth Day of September in the Year of our Lord one thousand seven hundred and Eighty seven and of the Independence of the United States of America the Twelfth

IN WITNESS whereof We have hereunto subscribed our Names,

G^o^. WASHINGTON—Presid^t^.
and deputy from Virginia

[Signed also by the deputies of twelve States.]

Delaware

GEO: READ
GUNNING BEDFORD JUN
JOHN DICKINSON
RICHARD BASSETT
JACO: BROOM

Maryland

JAMES McHENRY
DAN OF ST THOS JENIFER
DANL CARROLL

Virginia

JOHN BLAIR
JAMES MADISON JR.

North Carolina

WM BLOUNT
RICHD. DOBBS SPAIGHT
HU WILLIAMSON

South Carolina

J. RUTLEDGE
CHARLES COTESWORTH PINCKNEY
CHARLES PINCKNEY
PIERCE BUTLER

Georgia

WILLIAM FEW
ABR BALDWIN

New Hampshire

JOHN LANGDON
NICHOLAS GILMAN

Massachusetts

NATHANIEL GORHAM
RUFUS KING

Connecticut

WM. SAML. JOHNSON
ROGER SHERMAN

New York

ALEXANDER HAMILTON

New Jersey

WIL: LIVINGSTON
DAVID BREARLEY
WM. PATERSON
JONA: DAYTON

Pennsylvania

B FRANKLIN
THOMAS MIFFLIN
ROBT MORRIS
GEO. CLYMER
THOS. FITZSIMONS
JARED INGERSOLL
JAMES WILSON
GOUV MORRIS

Attest: WILLIAM JACKSON *Secretary*

ARTICLES IN ADDITION TO, AND AMENDMENT OF, THE CONSTITUTION OF THE UNITED STATES OF AMERICA, PROPOSED BY CONGRESS, AND RATIFIED BY THE LEGISLATURES OF THE SEVERAL STATES, PURSUANT TO THE FIFTH ARTICLE OF THE ORIGINAL CONSTITUTION [12]

ARTICLE [I.] [13]

Congress shall make no law respecting an establishment of religion, or prohibiting the free exercise thereof; or abridging the freedom of speech, or of the press; of the right of the people peaceably to assemble, and to petition the Government for a redress of grievances.

ARTICLE [II.]

A well regulated Militia, being necessary to the security of a free State, the right of the people to keep and bear Arms, shall not be infringed.

ARTICLE [III.]

No Soldier shall, in time of peace be quartered in any house, without the consent of the Owner, nor in time of war, but in a manner to be prescribed by law.

ARTICLE [IV.]

The right of the people to be secure in their persons, houses, papers, and effects, against unreasonable searches and seizures, shall not be violated, and no Warrants shall issue, but upon probable cause, supported by Oath or affirmation, and particularly describing the place to be searched, and the persons or things to be seized.

ARTICLE [V.]

No person shall be held to answer for a capital, or otherwise infamous crime, unless on a presentment or indictment of a Grand Jury, except in cases arising in the land or naval forces, or in the

[12] The first ten amendments of the Constitution of the United States (and two others, one of which failed of ratification and the other which later became the 27th amendment) were proposed to the legislatures of the several States by the First Congress on September 25, 1789. The first ten amendments were ratified by the following States, and the notifications of ratification by the Governors thereof were successively communicated by the President to Congress: New Jersey, November 20, 1789; Maryland, December 19, 1789; North Carolina, December 22, 1789; South Carolina, January 19, 1790; New Hampshire, January 25, 1790; Delaware, January 28, 1790; New York, February 24, 1790; Pennsylvania, March 10, 1790; Rhode Island, June 7, 1790; Vermont, November 3, 1791; and Virginia, December 15, 1791.

Ratification was completed on December 15, 1791.

The amendments were subsequently ratified by the legislatures of Massachusetts, March 2, 1939; Georgia, March 18, 1939; and Connecticut, April 19, 1939.

[13] Only the 13th, 14th, 15th, and 16th articles of amendment had numbers assigned to them at the time of ratification.

Militia, when in actual service in time of War or public danger; nor shall any person be subject for the same offence to be twice put in jeopardy of life or limb; nor shall be compelled in any criminal case to be a witness against himself, nor be deprived of life, liberty, or property, without due process of law; nor shall private property be taken for public use, without just compensation.

Article [VI.]

In all criminal prosecutions, the accused shall enjoy the right to a speedy and public trial, by an impartial jury of the State and district wherein the crime shall have been committed, which district shall have been previously ascertained by law, and to be informed of the nature and cause of the accusation; to be confronted with the witnesses against him; to have compulsory process for obtaining witnesses in his favor, and to have the Assistance of Counsel for his defense.

Article [VII.]

In Suits at common law, where the value in controversy shall exceed twenty dollars, the right of trial by jury shall be preserved, and no fact tried by a jury, shall be otherwise re-examined in any Court of the United States, than according to the rules of the common law.

Article [VIII.]

Excessive bail shall not be required, nor excessive fines imposed, nor cruel and unusual punishments inflicted.

Article [IX.]

The enumeration in the Constitution, of certain rights, shall not be construed to deny or disparage others retained by the people.

Article [X.]

The powers not delegated to the United States by the Constitution, nor prohibited by it to the States, are reserved to the States respectively, or to the people.

Article [XI.]

The Judicial power of the United States shall not be construed to extend to any suit in law or equity, commenced or prosecuted against one of the United States by Citizens of another State, or by Citizens or Subjects of any Foreign State.

Proposal and Ratification

The eleventh amendment to the Constitution of the United States was proposed to the legislatures of the several States by the Third Congress, on the 4th of March 1794; and was declared in a message from the President to Congress, dated the 8th of January, 1798, to have been ratified by the legislatures of three-fourths of the States. The dates of ratification were: New York, March 27, 1794; Rhode Island, March 31, 1794; Connecticut, May 8, 1794; New Hampshire, June 16, 1794; Massachusetts, June 26, 1794; Vermont, between October 9, 1794 and November 9, 1794; Virginia, November 18, 1794; Georgia, November 29, 1794; Kentucky, December 7,

1794; Maryland, December 26, 1794; Delaware, January 23, 1795; North Carolina, February 7, 1795.

Ratification was completed on February 7, 1795.

The amendment was subsequently ratified by South Carolina on December 4, 1797. New Jersey and Pennsylvania did not take action on the amendment.

ARTICLE [XII.]

The Electors shall meet in their respective states, and vote by ballot for President and Vice-President, one of whom, at least, shall not be an inhabitant of the same state with themselves; they shall name in their ballots the person voted for as President, and in distinct ballots the person voted for as Vice-President, and they shall make distinct lists of all persons voted for as President, and of all persons voted for as Vice-President, and of the number of votes for each, which lists they shall sign and certify, and transmit sealed to the seat of the government of the United States, directed to the President of the Senate;—The President of the Senate shall, in the presence of the Senate and House of Representatives, open all the certificates and the votes shall then be counted;—The person having the greatest number of votes for President, shall be the President, if such number be a majority of the whole number of Electors appointed; and if no person have such majority, then from the persons having the highest numbers not exceeding three on the list of those voted for as President, the House of Representatives shall choose immediately, by ballot, the President. But in choosing the President, the votes shall be taken by states, the representation from each state having one vote; a quorum for this purpose shall consist of a member or members from two-thirds of the states, and a majority of all the states shall be necessary to a choice. And if the House of Representatives shall not choose a President whenever the right of choice shall devolve upon them, before the fourth day of March next following, then the Vice-President shall act as President, as in the case of the death or other constitutional disability of the President.[14]—The person having the greatest number of votes as Vice-President, shall be the Vice-President, if such number be a majority of the whole number of Electors appointed, and if no person have a majority, then from the two highest numbers on the list, the Senate shall choose the Vice-President; a quorum for the purpose shall consist of two-thirds of the whole number of Senators, and a majority of the whole number shall be necessary to a choice. But no person constitutionally ineligible to the office of President shall be eligible to that of Vice-President of the United States.

PROPOSAL AND RATIFICATION

The twelfth amendment to the Constitution of the United States was proposed to the legislatures of the several States by the Eighth Congress, on the 9th of December, 1803, in lieu of the original third paragraph of the first section of the second article; and was declared in a proclamation of the Secretary of State, dated the 25th of September, 1804, to have been ratified by the legislatures of 13 of the 17 States. The dates of ratification were: North Carolina, December 21, 1803; Maryland, December 24, 1803; Kentucky, December 27, 1803; Ohio, December 30, 1803; Pennsylvania, January 5, 1804; Vermont, January 30, 1804; Virginia, February 3, 1804; New York, February 10, 1804; New Jersey, February 22, 1804; Rhode Island, March

[14] This sentence has been superseded by section 3 of amendment XX.

12, 1804; South Carolina, May 15, 1804; Georgia, May 19, 1804; New Hampshire, June 15, 1804.

Ratification was completed on June 15, 1804.

The amendment was subsequently ratified by Tennessee, July 27, 1804.

The amendment was rejected by Delaware, January 18, 1804; Massachusetts, February 3, 1804; Connecticut, at its session begun May 10, 1804.

ARTICLE XIII.

SECTION 1. Neither slavery nor involuntary servitude, except as a punishment for crime whereof the party shall have been duly convicted, shall exist within the United States, or any place subject to their jurisdiction.

SECTION 2. Congress shall have power to enforce this article by appropriate legislation.

PROPOSAL AND RATIFICATION

The thirteenth amendment to the Constitution of the United States was proposed to the legislatures of the several States by the Thirty-eighth Congress, on the 31st day of January, 1865, and was declared, in a proclamation of the Secretary of State, dated the 18th of December, 1865, to have been ratified by the legislatures of twenty-seven of the thirty-six States. The dates of ratification were: Illinois, February 1, 1865; Rhode Island, February 2, 1865; Michigan, February 2, 1865; Maryland, February 3, 1865; New York, February 3, 1865; Pennsylvania, February 3, 1865; West Virginia, February 3, 1865; Missouri, February 6, 1865; Maine, February 7, 1865; Kansas, February 7, 1865; Massachusetts, February 7, 1865; Virginia, February 9, 1865; Ohio, February 10, 1865; Indiana, February 13, 1865; Nevada, February 16, 1865; Louisiana, February 17, 1865; Minnesota, February 23, 1865; Wisconsin, February 24, 1865; Vermont, March 9, 1865; Tennessee, April 7, 1865; Arkansas, April 14, 1865; Connecticut, May 4, 1865; New Hampshire, July 1, 1865; South Carolina, November 13, 1865; Alabama, December 2, 1865; North Carolina, December 4, 1865; Georgia, December 6, 1865.

Ratification was completed on December 6, 1865.

The amendment was subsequently ratified by Oregon, December 8, 1865; California, December 19, 1865; Florida, December 28, 1865 (Florida again ratified on June 9, 1868, upon its adoption of a new constitution); Iowa, January 15, 1866; New Jersey, January 23, 1866 (after having rejected the amendment on March 16, 1865); Texas, February 18, 1870; Delaware, February 12, 1901 (after having rejected the amendment on February 8, 1865); Kentucky, March 18, 1976 (after having rejected it on February 24, 1865).

The amendment was rejected (and not subsequently ratified) by Mississippi, December 4, 1865.

ARTICLE XIV.

SECTION 1. All persons born or naturalized in the United States, and subject to the jurisdiction thereof, are citizens of the United States and of the State wherein they reside. No State shall make or enforce any law which shall abridge the privileges or immunities of citizens of the United States; nor shall any State deprive any person of life, liberty, or property, without due process of law; nor deny to any person within its jurisdiction the equal protection of the laws.

SECTION 2. Representatives shall be apportioned among the several States according to their respective numbers, counting the whole number of persons in each State, excluding Indians not taxed. But when the right to vote at any election for the choice of electors for President and Vice President of the United States, Representatives in Congress, the Executive and Judicial officers of a State, or the members of the Legislature thereof, is denied to any of the male inhabitants of such State, being twenty-one years of age,[15] and citizens of the United States, or in any way abridged, except for participation in rebellion, or other crime, the basis of representation therein shall be reduced in the proportion which the number of such male citizens shall bear to the whole number of male citizens twenty-one years of age in such State.

SECTION 3. No person shall be a Senator or Representative in Congress, or elector of President and Vice President, or hold any office, civil or military, under the United States, or under any State, who, having previously taken an oath, as a member of Congress, or as an officer of the United States, or as a member of any State legislature, or as an executive or judicial officer of any State, to support the Constitution of the United States, shall have engaged in insurrection or rebellion against the same, or given aid or comfort to the enemies thereof. But Congress may by a vote of two-thirds of each House, remove such disability.

SECTION 4. The validity of the public debt of the United States, authorized by law, including debts incurred for payment of pensions and bounties for services in suppressing insurrection or rebellion, shall not be questioned. But neither the United States nor any State shall assume or pay any debt or obligation incurred in aid of insurrection or rebellion against the United States, or any claim for the loss or emancipation of any slave; but all such debts, obligations and claims shall be held illegal and void.

SECTION 5. The Congress shall have power to enforce, by appropriate legislation, the provisions of this article.

PROPOSAL AND RATIFICATION

The fourteenth amendment to the Constitution of the United States was proposed to the legislatures of the several States by the Thirty-ninth Congress, on the 13th of June, 1866. It was declared, in a certificate of the Secretary of State dated July 28, 1868 to have been ratified by the legislatures of 28 of the 37 States. The dates of ratification were: Connecticut, June 25, 1866; New Hampshire, July 6, 1866; Tennessee, July 19, 1866; New Jersey, September 11, 1866 (subsequently the legislature rescinded its ratification, and on March 24, 1868, readopted its resolution of rescission over the Governor's veto, and on November 12, 1980, expressed support for the amendment); Oregon, September 19, 1866 (and rescinded its ratification on October 15, 1868); Vermont, October 30, 1866; Ohio, January 4, 1867 (and rescinded its ratification on January 15, 1868); New York, January 10, 1867; Kansas, January 11, 1867; Illinois, January 15, 1867; West Virginia, January 16, 1867; Michigan, January 16, 1867; Minnesota, January 16, 1867; Maine, January 19, 1867; Nevada, January 22, 1867; Indiana, January 23, 1867; Missouri, January 25, 1867; Rhode Island, February 7, 1867; Wisconsin, February 7, 1867; Pennsylvania, February 12, 1867; Massachusetts, March 20, 1867; Nebraska, June 15, 1867; Iowa, March 16, 1868; Arkansas, April 6, 1868; Florida, June 9, 1868; North Carolina, July 4, 1868 (after having rejected it on December 14, 1866); Louisiana, July 9, 1868 (after having rejected it on February 6, 1867); South Carolina, July 9, 1868 (after having rejected it on December 20, 1866).

Ratification was completed on July 9, 1868.

The amendment was subsequently ratified by Alabama, July 13, 1868; Georgia, July 21, 1868 (after having rejected it on November 9, 1866); Virginia, October 8, 1869 (after having rejected it on January 9, 1867); Mississippi, January 17, 1870; Texas, February 18, 1870 (after having rejected it on October 27, 1866); Delaware, February 12, 1901 (after having rejected it on February 8, 1867); Maryland, April 4, 1959 (after having rejected it on March 23, 1867); California, May 6, 1959; Kentucky, March 18, 1976 (after having rejected it on January 8, 1867).

[15] See amendment XIX and section 1 of amendment XXVI.

ARTICLE XV.

SECTION 1. The right of citizens of the United States to vote shall not be denied or abridged by the United States or by any State on account of race, color, or previous condition of servitude.

SECTION 2. The Congress shall have power to enforce this article by appropriate legislation.

PROPOSAL AND RATIFICATION

The fifteenth amendment to the Constitution of the United States was proposed to the legislatures of the several States by the Fortieth Congress, on the 26th of February, 1869, and was declared, in a proclamation of the Secretary of State, dated March 30, 1870, to have been ratified by the legislatures of twenty-nine of the thirty-seven States. The dates of ratification were: Nevada, March 1, 1869; West Virginia, March 3, 1869; Illinois, March 5, 1869; Louisiana, March 5, 1869; North Carolina, March 5, 1869; Michigan, March 8, 1869; Wisconsin, March 9, 1869; Maine, March 11, 1869; Massachusetts, March 12, 1869; Arkansas, March 15, 1869; South Carolina, March 15, 1869; Pennsylvania, March 25, 1869; New York, April 14, 1869 (and the legislature of the same State passed a resolution January 5, 1870, to withdraw its consent to it, which action it rescinded on March 30, 1970); Indiana, May 14, 1869; Connecticut, May 19, 1869; Florida, June 14, 1869; New Hampshire, July 1, 1869; Virginia, October 8, 1869; Vermont, October 20, 1869; Missouri, January 7, 1870; Minnesota, January 13, 1870; Mississippi, January 17, 1870; Rhode Island, January 18, 1870; Kansas, January 19, 1870; Ohio, January 27, 1870 (after having rejected it on April 30, 1869); Georgia, February 2, 1870; Iowa, February 3, 1870.

Ratification was completed on February 3, 1870, unless the withdrawal of ratification by New York was effective; in which event ratification was completed on February 17, 1870, when Nebraska ratified.

The amendment was subsequently ratified by Texas, February 18, 1870; New Jersey, February 15, 1871 (after having rejected it on February 7, 1870); Delaware, February 12, 1901 (after having rejected it on March 18, 1869); Oregon, February 24, 1959; California, April 3, 1962 (after having rejected it on January 28, 1870); Kentucky, March 18, 1976 (after having rejected it on March 12, 1869); Tennessee, April 8, 1997 (after having rejected it on November 16, 1869).

The amendment was approved by the Governor of Maryland, May 7, 1973; Maryland having previously rejected it on February 26, 1870.

ARTICLE XVI.

The Congress shall have power to lay and collect taxes on incomes, from whatever source derived, without apportionment among the several States, and without regard to any census or enumeration.

PROPOSAL AND RATIFICATION

The sixteenth amendment to the Constitution of the United States was proposed to the legislatures of the several States by the Sixty-first Congress on the 12th of July, 1909, and was declared, in a proclamation of the Secretary of State, dated the 25th of February, 1913, to have been ratified by 36 of the 48 States. The dates of ratification were: Alabama, August 10, 1909; Kentucky, February 8, 1910; South Carolina, February 19, 1910; Illinois, March 1, 1910; Mississippi, March 7, 1910; Oklahoma, March 10, 1910; Maryland, April 8, 1910; Georgia, August 3, 1910; Texas, August 16, 1910; Ohio, January 19, 1911; Idaho, January 20, 1911; Oregon, January 23, 1911; Washington, January 26, 1911; Montana, January 30, 1911; Indiana, January 30, 1911; California, January 31, 1911; Nevada, January 31, 1911; South Dakota, February 3, 1911; Nebraska, February 9, 1911; North Carolina, February 11, 1911; Colorado, February 15, 1911; North Dakota, February 17, 1911; Kansas, February 18, 1911; Michigan, February 23, 1911; Iowa, February 24, 1911; Missouri, March 16, 1911; Maine, March 31, 1911; Tennessee, April 7, 1911; Arkansas, April 22, 1911 (after having rejected it earlier); Wisconsin, May 26, 1911; New York, July 12, 1911; Arizona, April 6, 1912; Minnesota, June 11, 1912; Louisiana, June 28, 1912; West Virginia, January 31, 1913; New Mexico, February 3, 1913.

Ratification was completed on February 3, 1913.

The amendment was subsequently ratified by Massachusetts, March 4, 1913; New Hampshire, March 7, 1913 (after having rejected it on March 2, 1911).

The amendment was rejected (and not subsequently ratified) by Connecticut, Rhode Island, and Utah.

ARTICLE [XVII.]

The Senate of the United States shall be composed of two Senators from each State, elected by the people thereof, for six years; and each Senator shall have one vote. The electors in each State shall have the qualifications requisite for electors of the most numerous branch of the State legislatures.

When vacancies happen in the representation of any State in the Senate, the executive authority of such State shall issue writs of election to fill such vacancies: Provided, That the legislature of any State may empower the executive thereof to make temporary appointments until the people fill the vacancies by election as the legislature may direct.

This amendment shall not be so construed as to affect the election or term of any Senator chosen before it becomes valid as part of the Constitution.

PROPOSAL AND RATIFICATION

The seventeenth amendment to the Constitution of the United States was proposed to the legislatures of the several States by the Sixty-second Congress on the 13th of May, 1912, and was declared, in a proclamation of the Secretary of State, dated the 31st of May, 1913, to have been ratified by the legislatures of 36 of the 48 States. The dates of ratification were: Massachusetts, May 22, 1912; Arizona, June 3, 1912; Minnesota, June 10, 1912; New York, January 15, 1913; Kansas, January 17, 1913; Oregon, January 23, 1913; North Carolina, January 25, 1913; California, January 28, 1913; Michigan, January 28, 1913; Iowa, January 30, 1913; Montana, January 30, 1913; Idaho, January 31, 1913; West Virginia, February 4, 1913; Colorado, February 5, 1913; Nevada, February 6, 1913; Texas, February 7, 1913; Washington, February 7, 1913; Wyoming, February 8, 1913; Arkansas, February 11, 1913; Maine, February 11, 1913; Illinois, February 13, 1913; North Dakota, February 14, 1913; Wisconsin, February 18, 1913; Indiana, February 19, 1913; New Hampshire, February 19, 1913; Vermont, February 19, 1913; South Dakota, February 19, 1913; Oklahoma, February 24, 1913; Ohio, February 25, 1913; Missouri, March 7, 1913; New Mexico, March 13, 1913; Nebraska, March 14, 1913; New Jersey, March 17, 1913; Tennessee, April 1, 1913; Pennsylvania, April 2, 1913; Connecticut, April 8, 1913.

Ratification was completed on April 8, 1913.

The amendment was subsequently ratified by Louisiana, June 11, 1914.

The amendment was rejected by Utah (and not subsequently ratified) on February 26, 1913.

ARTICLE [XVIII.] [16]

SECTION 1. After one year from the ratification of this article the manufacture, sale, or transportation of intoxicating liquors within, the importation thereof into, or the exportation thereof from the United States and all territory subject to the jurisdiction thereof for beverage purposes is hereby prohibited.

SECTION 2. The Congress and the several States shall have concurrent power to enforce this article by appropriate legislation.

SECTION 3. This article shall be inoperative unless it shall have been ratified as an amendment to the Constitution by the legislatures of the several States, as provided in the Constitution, within

[16] Repealed by section 1 of amendment XXI.

seven years from the date of the submission hereof to the States by the Congress.

PROPOSAL AND RATIFICATION

The eighteenth amendment to the Constitution of the United States was proposed to the legislatures of the several States by the Sixty-fifth Congress, on the 18th of December, 1917, and was declared, in a proclamation of the Secretary of State, dated the 29th of January, 1919, to have been ratified by the legislatures of 36 of the 48 States. The dates of ratification were: Mississippi, January 8, 1918; Virginia, January 11, 1918; Kentucky, January 14, 1918; North Dakota, January 25, 1918; South Carolina, January 29, 1918; Maryland, February 13, 1918; Montana, February 19, 1918; Texas, March 4, 1918; Delaware, March 18, 1918; South Dakota, March 20, 1918; Massachusetts, April 2, 1918; Arizona, May 24, 1918; Georgia, June 26, 1918; Louisiana, August 3, 1918; Florida, December 3, 1918; Michigan, January 2, 1919; Ohio, January 7, 1919; Oklahoma, January 7, 1919; Idaho, January 8, 1919; Maine, January 8, 1919; West Virginia, January 9, 1919; California, January 13, 1919; Tennessee, January 13, 1919; Washington, January 13, 1919; Arkansas, January 14, 1919; Kansas, January 14, 1919; Alabama, January 15, 1919; Colorado, January 15, 1919; Iowa, January 15, 1919; New Hampshire, January 15, 1919; Oregon, January 15, 1919; Nebraska, January 16, 1919; North Carolina, January 16, 1919; Utah, January 16, 1919; Missouri, January 16, 1919; Wyoming, January 16, 1919.

Ratification was completed on January 16, 1919. See Dillon v. Gloss, 256 U.S. 368, 376 (1921).

The amendment was subsequently ratified by Minnesota on January 17, 1919; Wisconsin, January 17, 1919; New Mexico, January 20, 1919; Nevada, January 21, 1919; New York, January 29, 1919; Vermont, January 29, 1919; Pennsylvania, February 25, 1919; Connecticut, May 6, 1919; and New Jersey, March 9, 1922.

The amendment was rejected (and not subsequently ratified) by Rhode Island.

ARTICLE [XIX.]

The right of citizens of the United States to vote shall not be denied or abridged by the United States or by any State on account of sex.

Congress shall have power to enforce this article by appropriate legislation.

PROPOSAL AND RATIFICATION

The nineteenth amendment to the Constitution of the United States was proposed to the legislatures of the several States by the Sixty-sixth Congress, on the 4th of June, 1919, and was declared, in a proclamation of the Secretary of State, dated the 26th of August, 1920, to have been ratified by the legislatures of 36 of the 48 States. The dates of ratification were: Illinois, June 10, 1919 (and that State readopted its resolution of ratification June 17, 1919); Michigan, June 10, 1919; Wisconsin, June 10, 1919; Kansas, June 16, 1919; New York, June 16, 1919; Ohio, June 16, 1919; Pennsylvania, June 24, 1919; Massachusetts, June 25, 1919; Texas, June 28, 1919; Iowa, July 2, 1919; Missouri, July 3, 1919; Arkansas, July 28, 1919; Montana, August 2, 1919; Nebraska, August 2, 1919; Minnesota, September 8, 1919; New Hampshire, September 10, 1919; Utah, October 2, 1919; California, November 1, 1919; Maine, November 5, 1919; North Dakota, December 1, 1919; South Dakota, December 4, 1919; Colorado, December 15, 1919; Kentucky, January 6, 1920; Rhode Island, January 6, 1920; Oregon, January 13, 1920; Indiana, January 16, 1920; Wyoming, January 27, 1920; Nevada, February 7, 1920; New Jersey, February 9, 1920; Idaho, February 11, 1920; Arizona, February 12, 1920; New Mexico, February 21, 1920; Oklahoma, February 28, 1920; West Virginia, March 10, 1920; Washington, March 22, 1920; Tennessee, August 18, 1920.

Ratification was completed on August 18, 1920.

The amendment was subsequently ratified by Connecticut on September 14, 1920 (and that State reaffirmed it on September 21, 1920); Vermont, February 8, 1921; Delaware, March 6, 1923 (after having rejected it on June 2, 1920); Maryland, March 29, 1941 (after having rejected it on February 24, 1920, ratification certified on February 25, 1958); Virginia, February 21, 1952 (after having rejected it on February 12, 1920); Alabama, September 8, 1953 (after having rejected it on September 22, 1919); Florida, May 13, 1969; South Carolina, July 1, 1969 (after having rejected it on January 28, 1920, ratification certified on August 22, 1973); Georgia, February

20, 1970 (after having rejected it on July 24, 1919); Louisiana, June 11, 1970 (after having rejected it on July 1, 1920); North Carolina, May 6, 1971; Mississippi, March 22, 1984 (after having rejected it on March 29, 1920).

ARTICLE [XX.]

SECTION 1. The terms of the President and Vice President shall end at noon on the 20th day of January, and the terms of Senators and Representatives at noon on the 3d day of January, of the years in which such terms would have ended if this article had not been ratified; and the terms of their successors shall then begin.

SECTION 2. The Congress shall assemble at least once in every year, and such meeting shall begin at noon on the 3d day of January, unless they shall by law appoint a different day.

SECTION 3. If, at the time fixed for the beginning of the term of the President, the President elect shall have died, the Vice President elect shall become President. If a President shall not have been chosen before the time fixed for the beginning of his term, or if the President elect shall have failed to qualify, then the Vice President elect shall act as President until a President shall have qualified; and the Congress may by law provide for the case wherein neither a President elect nor a Vice President elect shall have qualified, declaring who shall then act as President, or the manner in which one who is to act shall be selected, and such person shall act accordingly until a President or Vice President shall have qualified.

SECTION 4. The Congress may by law provide for the case of the death of any of the persons from whom the House of Representatives may choose a President whenever the right of choice shall have devolved upon them, and for the case of the death of any of the persons from whom the Senate may choose a Vice President whenever the right of choice shall have devolved upon them.

SECTION 5. Sections 1 and 2 shall take effect on the 15th day of October following the ratification of this article.

SECTION 6. This article shall be inoperative unless it shall have been ratified as an amendment to the Constitution by the legislatures of three-fourths of the several States within seven years from the date of its submission.

PROPOSAL AND RATIFICATION

The twentieth amendment to the Constitution was proposed to the legislatures of the several states by the Seventy-Second Congress, on the 2d day of March, 1932, and was declared, in a proclamation by the Secretary of State, dated on the 6th day of February, 1933, to have been ratified by the legislatures of 36 of the 48 States. The dates of ratification were: Virginia, March 4, 1932; New York, March 11, 1932; Mississippi, March 16, 1932; Arkansas, March 17, 1932; Kentucky, March 17, 1932; New Jersey, March 21, 1932; South Carolina, March 25, 1932; Michigan, March 31, 1932; Maine, April 1, 1932; Rhode Island, April 14, 1932; Illinois, April 21, 1932; Louisiana, June 22, 1932; West Virginia, July 30, 1932; Pennsylvania, August 11, 1932; Indiana, August 15, 1932; Texas, September 7, 1932; Alabama, September 13, 1932; California, January 4, 1933; North Carolina, January 5, 1933; North Dakota, January 9, 1933; Minnesota, January 12, 1933; Arizona, January 13, 1933; Montana, January 13, 1933; Nebraska, January 13, 1933; Oklahoma, January 13, 1933; Kansas, January 16, 1933; Oregon, January 16, 1933; Delaware, January 19, 1933; Washington, January 19, 1933; Wyoming, January 19, 1933; Iowa, January 20, 1933; South Dakota, January 20, 1933; Tennessee, January 20, 1933; Idaho, January 21, 1933; New Mexico, January 21, 1933; Georgia, January 23, 1933; Missouri, January 23, 1933; Ohio, January 23, 1933; Utah, January 23, 1933.

Ratification was completed on January 23, 1933.

The amendment was subsequently ratified by Massachusetts on January 24, 1933; Wisconsin, January 24, 1933; Colorado, January 24, 1933; Nevada, January 26, 1933; Connecticut, January 27, 1933; New Hampshire, January 31, 1933; Vermont, February 2, 1933; Maryland, March 24, 1933; Florida, April 26, 1933.

ARTICLE [XXI.]

SECTION 1. The eighteenth article of amendment to the Constitution of the United States is hereby repealed.

SECTION 2. The transportation or importation into any State, Territory, or possession of the United States for delivery or use therein of intoxicating liquors, in violation of the laws thereof, is hereby prohibited.

SECTION 3. This article shall be inoperative unless it shall have been ratified as an amendment to the Constitution by conventions in the several States, as provided in the Constitution, within seven years from the date of the submission hereof to the States by the Congress.

PROPOSAL AND RATIFICATION

The twenty-first amendment to the Constitution was proposed to the several states by the Seventy-Second Congress, on the 20th day of February, 1933, and was declared, in a proclamation by the Secretary of State, dated on the 5th day of December, 1933, to have been ratified by 36 of the 48 States. The dates of ratification were: Michigan, April 10, 1933; Wisconsin, April 25, 1933; Rhode Island, May 8, 1933; Wyoming, May 25, 1933; New Jersey, June 1, 1933; Delaware, June 24, 1933; Indiana, June 26, 1933; Massachusetts, June 26, 1933; New York, June 27, 1933; Illinois, July 10, 1933; Iowa, July 10, 1933; Connecticut, July 11, 1933; New Hampshire, July 11, 1933; California, July 24, 1933; West Virginia, July 25, 1933; Arkansas, August 1, 1933; Oregon, August 7, 1933; Alabama, August 8, 1933; Tennessee, August 11, 1933; Missouri, August 29, 1933; Arizona, September 5, 1933; Nevada, September 5, 1933; Vermont, September 23, 1933; Colorado, September 26, 1933; Washington, October 3, 1933; Minnesota, October 10, 1933; Idaho, October 17, 1933, Maryland, October 18, 1933; Virginia, October 25, 1933; New Mexico, November 2, 1933; Florida, November 14, 1933; Texas, November 24, 1933; Kentucky, November 27, 1933; Ohio, December 5, 1933; Pennsylvania, December 5, 1933; Utah, December 5, 1933.

Ratification was completed on December 5, 1933.

The amendment was subsequently ratified by Maine, on December 6, 1933, and by Montana, on August 6, 1934.

The amendment was rejected (and not subsequently ratified) by South Carolina, on December 4, 1933.

ARTICLE [XXII.]

SECTION 1. No person shall be elected to the office of the President more than twice, and no person who has held the office of President, or acted as President, for more than two years of a term of which some other person was elected President shall be elected to the office of the President more than once. But this Article shall not apply to any person holding the office of President when this Article was proposed by the Congress, and shall not prevent any person who may be holding the office of President, or acting as President, during the term within which this Article becomes operative from holding the office of President or acting as President during the remainder of such term.

SECTION 2. This article shall be inoperative unless it shall have been ratified as an amendment to the Constitution by the legislatures of three-fourths of the several States within seven years from the date of its submission to the States by the Congress.

PROPOSAL AND RATIFICATION

This amendment was proposed to the legislatures of the several States by the Eightieth Congress on March 21, 1947 by House Joint Res. No. 27, and was declared by the Administrator of General Services, on March 1, 1951, to have been ratified by the legislatures of 36 of the 48 States. The dates of ratification were: Maine, March 31, 1947; Michigan, March 31, 1947; Iowa, April 1, 1947; Kansas, April 1, 1947; New Hampshire, April 1, 1947; Delaware, April 2, 1947; Illinois, April 3, 1947; Oregon, April 3, 1947; Colorado, April 12, 1947; California, April 15, 1947; New Jersey, April 15, 1947; Vermont, April 15, 1947; Ohio, April 16, 1947; Wisconsin, April 16, 1947; Pennsylvania, April 29, 1947; Connecticut, May 21, 1947; Missouri, May 22, 1947; Nebraska, May 23, 1947; Virginia, January 28, 1948; Mississippi, February 12, 1948; New York, March 9, 1948; South Dakota, January 21, 1949; North Dakota, February 25, 1949; Louisiana, May 17, 1950; Montana, January 25, 1951; Indiana, January 29, 1951; Idaho, January 30, 1951; New Mexico, February 12, 1951; Wyoming, February 12, 1951; Arkansas, February 15, 1951; Georgia, February 17, 1951; Tennessee, February 20, 1951; Texas, February 22, 1951; Nevada, February 26, 1951; Utah, February 26, 1951; Minnesota, February 27, 1951.

Ratification was completed on February 27, 1951.

The amendment was subsequently ratified by North Carolina on February 28, 1951; South Carolina, March 13, 1951; Maryland, March 14, 1951; Florida, April 16, 1951; Alabama, May 4, 1951.

The amendment was rejected (and not subsequently ratified) by Oklahoma in June 1947, and Massachusetts on June 9, 1949.

CERTIFICATION OF VALIDITY

Publication of the certifying statement of the Administrator of General Services that the amendment had become valid was made on March 1, 1951, F.R. Doc. 51–2940, 16 F.R. 2019.

ARTICLE [XXIII.]

SECTION 1. The District constituting the seat of Government of the United States shall appoint in such manner as the Congress may direct:

A number of electors of President and Vice President equal to the whole number of Senators and Representatives in Congress to which the District would be entitled if it were a State, but in no event more than the least populous State; they shall be in addition to those appointed by the States, but they shall be considered, for the purposes of the election of President and Vice President, to be electors appointed by a State; and they shall meet in the District and perform such duties as provided by the twelfth article of amendment.

SECTION 2. The Congress shall have power to enforce this article by appropriate legislation.

PROPOSAL AND RATIFICATION

This amendment was proposed by the Eighty-sixth Congress on June 17, 1960 and was declared by the Administrator of General Services on April 3, 1961, to have been ratified by 38 of the 50 States. The dates of ratification were: Hawaii, June 23, 1960 (and that State made a technical correction to its resolution on June 30, 1960); Massachusetts, August 22, 1960; New Jersey, December 19, 1960; New York, January 17, 1961; California, January 19, 1961; Oregon, January 27, 1961; Maryland, January 30, 1961; Idaho, January 31, 1961; Maine, January 31, 1961; Minnesota, January 31, 1961; New Mexico, February 1, 1961; Nevada, February 2, 1961; Montana, February 6, 1961; South Dakota, February 6, 1961; Colorado, February 8, 1961; Washington, February 9, 1961; West Virginia, February 9, 1961; Alaska, February 10, 1961; Wyoming, February 13, 1961; Delaware, February 20, 1961; Utah, February 21, 1961; Wisconsin, February 21, 1961; Pennsylvania, February 28, 1961; Indiana, March 3, 1961; North Dakota, March 3, 1961; Tennessee, March 6, 1961; Michigan, March 8, 1961; Connecticut, March 9, 1961; Arizona, March 10, 1961; Illinois, March 14, 1961; Nebraska, March 15, 1961; Vermont, March 15, 1961;

Iowa, March 16, 1961; Missouri, March 20, 1961; Oklahoma, March 21, 1961; Rhode Island, March 22, 1961; Kansas, March 29, 1961; Ohio, March 29, 1961.

Ratification was completed on March 29, 1961.

The amendment was subsequently ratified by New Hampshire on March 30, 1961 (when that State annulled and then repeated its ratification of March 29, 1961).

The amendment was rejected (and not subsequently ratified) by Arkansas on January 24, 1961.

CERTIFICATION OF VALIDITY

Publication of the certifying statement of the Administrator of General Services that the amendment had become valid was made on April 3, 1961, F.R. Doc. 61–3017, 26 F.R. 2808.

ARTICLE [XXIV.]

SECTION 1. The right of citizens of the United States to vote in any primary or other election for President or Vice President, for electors for President or Vice President, or for Senator or Representative in Congress, shall not be denied or abridged by the United States or any State by reason of failure to pay any poll tax or other tax.

SECTION 2. The Congress shall have power to enforce this article by appropriate legislation.

PROPOSAL AND RATIFICATION

This amendment was proposed by the Eighty-seventh Congress by Senate Joint Resolution No. 29, which was approved by the Senate on March 27, 1962, and by the House of Representatives on August 27, 1962. It was declared by the Administrator of General Services on February 4, 1964, to have been ratified by the legislatures of 38 of the 50 States.

This amendment was ratified by the following States: Illinois, November 14, 1962; New Jersey, December 3, 1962; Oregon, January 25, 1963; Montana, January 28, 1963; West Virginia, February 1, 1963; New York, February 4, 1963; Maryland, February 6, 1963; California, February 7, 1963; Alaska, February 11, 1963; Rhode Island, February 14, 1963; Indiana, February 19, 1963; Utah, February 20, 1963; Michigan, February 20, 1963; Colorado, February 21, 1963; Ohio, February 27, 1963; Minnesota, February 27, 1963; New Mexico, March 5, 1963; Hawaii, March 6, 1963; North Dakota, March 7, 1963; Idaho, March 8, 1963; Washington, March 14, 1963; Vermont, March 15, 1963; Nevada, March 19, 1963; Connecticut, March 20, 1963; Tennessee, March 21, 1963; Pennsylvania, March 25, 1963; Wisconsin, March 26, 1963; Kansas, March 28, 1963; Massachusetts, March 28, 1963; Nebraska, April 4, 1963; Florida, April 18, 1963; Iowa, April 24, 1963; Delaware, May 1, 1963; Missouri, May 13, 1963; New Hampshire, June 12, 1963; Kentucky, June 27, 1963; Maine, January 16, 1964; South Dakota, January 23, 1964; Virginia, February 25, 1977.

Ratification was completed on January 23, 1964.

The amendment was subsequently ratified by North Carolina on May 3, 1989.

The amendment was rejected by Mississippi (and not subsequently ratified) on December 20, 1962.

CERTIFICATION OF VALIDITY

Publication of the certifying statement of the Administrator of General Services that the amendment had become valid was made on February 5, 1964, F.R. Doc. 64–1229, 29 F.R. 1715.

ARTICLE [XXV.]

SECTION 1. In case of the removal of the President from office or of his death or resignation, the Vice President shall become President.

SECTION 2. Whenever there is a vacancy in the office of the Vice President, the President shall nominate a Vice President who shall take office upon confirmation by a majority vote of both Houses of Congress.

SECTION 3. Whenever the President transmits to the President pro tempore of the Senate and the Speaker of the House of Representatives his written declaration that he is unable to discharge the powers and duties of his office, and until he transmits to them a written declaration to the contrary, such powers and duties shall be discharged by the Vice President as Acting President.

SECTION 4. Whenever the Vice President and a majority of either the principal officers of the executive departments or of such other body as Congress may by law provide, transmit to the President pro tempore of the Senate and the Speaker of the House of Representatives their written declaration that the President is unable to discharge the powers and duties of his office, the Vice President shall immediately assume the powers and duties of the office as Acting President.

Thereafter, when the President transmits to the President pro tempore of the Senate and the Speaker of the House of Representatives his written declaration that no inability exists, he shall resume the powers and duties of his office unless the Vice President and a majority of either the principal officers of the executive department[17] or of such other body as Congress may by law provide, transmit within four days to the President pro tempore of the Senate and the Speaker of the House of Representatives their written declaration that the President is unable to discharge the powers and duties of his office. Thereupon Congress shall decide the issue, assembling within forty-eight hours for that purpose if not in session. If the Congress, within twenty-one days after receipt of the latter written declaration, or, if Congress is not in session, within twenty-one days after Congress is required to assemble, determines by two-thirds vote of both Houses that the President is unable to discharge the powers and duties of his office, the Vice President shall continue to discharge the same as Acting President; otherwise, the President shall resume the powers and duties of his office.

PROPOSAL AND RATIFICATION

This amendment was proposed by the Eighty-ninth Congress by Senate Joint Resolution No. 1, which was approved by the Senate on February 19, 1965, and by the House of Representatives, in amended form, on April 13, 1965. The House of Representatives agreed to a Conference Report on June 30, 1965, and the Senate agreed to the Conference Report on July 6, 1965. It was declared by the Administrator of General Services, on February 23, 1967, to have been ratified by the legislatures of 39 of the 50 States.

This amendment was ratified by the following States: Nebraska, July 12, 1965; Wisconsin, July 13, 1965; Oklahoma, July 15, 1965; Massachusetts, August 9, 1965; Pennsylvania, August 18, 1965; Kentucky, September 15, 1965; Arizona, September 22, 1965; Michigan, October 5, 1965; Indiana, October 20, 1965; California, October 21, 1965; Arkansas, November 4, 1965; New Jersey, November 29, 1965; Delaware, December 7, 1965; Utah, January 17, 1966; West Virginia, January 20, 1966; Maine, January 24, 1966; Rhode Island, January 28, 1966; Colorado, February 3, 1966; New Mexico, February 3, 1966; Kansas, February 8, 1966; Vermont, February 10, 1966; Alaska, February 18, 1966; Idaho, March 2, 1966; Hawaii, March 3, 1966; Virginia, March 8, 1966; Mississippi, March 10, 1966; New York, March 14, 1966; Maryland, March 23, 1966; Missouri, March 30, 1966; New Hampshire, June 13, 1966; Louisiana, July 5, 1966; Tennessee, January 12, 1967; Wyoming, January 25, 1967;

[17] So in original. Probably should be "departments".

Washington, January 26, 1967; Iowa, January 26, 1967; Oregon, February 2, 1967; Minnesota, February 10, 1967; Nevada, February 10, 1967.

Ratification was completed on February 10, 1967.

The amendment was subsequently ratified by Connecticut, February 14, 1967; Montana, February 15, 1967; South Dakota, March 6, 1967; Ohio, March 7, 1967; Alabama, March 14, 1967; North Carolina, March 22, 1967; Illinois, March 22, 1967; Texas, April 25, 1967; Florida, May 25, 1967.

CERTIFICATION OF VALIDITY

Publication of the certifying statement of the Administrator of General Services that the amendment had become valid was made on February 25, 1967, F.R. Doc. 67–2208, 32 F.R. 3287.

ARTICLE [XXVI.]

SECTION 1. The right of citizens of the United States, who are eighteen years of age or older, to vote shall not be denied or abridged by the United States or by any State on account of age.

SECTION 2. The Congress shall have power to enforce this article by appropriate legislation.

PROPOSAL AND RATIFICATION

This amendment was proposed by the Ninety-second Congress by Senate Joint Resolution No. 7, which was approved by the Senate on March 10, 1971, and by the House of Representatives on March 23, 1971. It was declared by the Administrator of General Services on July 5, 1971, to have been ratified by the legislature of 39 of the 50 States.

This amendment was ratified by the following States: Connecticut, March 23, 1971; Delaware, March 23, 1971; Minnesota, March 23, 1971; Tennessee, March 23, 1971; Washington, March 23, 1971; Hawaii, March 24, 1971; Massachusetts, March 24, 1971; Montana, March 29, 1971; Arkansas, March 30, 1971; Idaho, March 30, 1971; Iowa, March 30, 1971; Nebraska, April 2, 1971; New Jersey, April 3, 1971; Kansas, April 7, 1971; Michigan, April 7, 1971; Alaska, April 8, 1971; Maryland, April 8, 1971; Indiana, April 8, 1971; Maine, April 9, 1971; Vermont, April 16, 1971; Louisiana, April 17, 1971; California, April 19, 1971; Colorado, April 27, 1971; Pennsylvania, April 27, 1971; Texas, April 27, 1971; South Carolina, April 28, 1971; West Virginia, April 28, 1971; New Hampshire, May 13, 1971; Arizona, May 14, 1971; Rhode Island, May 27, 1971; New York, June 2, 1971; Oregon, June 4, 1971; Missouri, June 14, 1971; Wisconsin, June 22, 1971; Illinois, June 29, 1971; Alabama, June 30, 1971; Ohio, June 30, 1971; North Carolina, July 1, 1971; Oklahoma, July 1, 1971.

Ratification was completed on July 1, 1971.

The amendment was subsequently ratified by Virginia, July 8, 1971; Wyoming, July 8, 1971; Georgia, October 4, 1971.

CERTIFICATION OF VALIDITY

Publication of the certifying statement of the Administrator of General Services that the amendment had become valid was made on July 7, 1971, F.R. Doc. 71–9691, 36 F.R. 12725.

ARTICLE [XXVII.]

No law, varying the compensation for the services of the Senators and Representatives, shall take effect, until an election of Representatives shall have intervened.

PROPOSAL AND RATIFICATION

This amendment, being the second of twelve articles proposed by the First Congress on Sept. 25, 1789, was declared by the Archivist of the United States on May 18, 1992, to have been ratified by the legislatures of 40 of the 50 States.

This amendment was ratified by the following States: Maryland, December 19, 1789; North Carolina, December 22, 1789; South Carolina, January 19, 1790; Delaware, January 28, 1790; Vermont, November 3, 1791; Virginia, December 15, 1791;

Ohio, May 6, 1873; Wyoming, March 6, 1978; Maine, April 27, 1983; Colorado, April 22, 1984; South Dakota, February 21, 1985; New Hampshire, March 7, 1985; Arizona, April 3, 1985; Tennessee, May 23, 1985; Oklahoma, July 10, 1985; New Mexico, February 14, 1986; Indiana, February 24, 1986; Utah, February 25, 1986; Arkansas, March 6, 1987; Montana, March 17, 1987; Connecticut, May 13, 1987; Wisconsin, July 15, 1987; Georgia, February 2, 1988; West Virginia, March 10, 1988; Louisiana, July 7, 1988; Iowa, February 9, 1989; Idaho, March 23, 1989; Nevada, April 26, 1989; Alaska, May 6, 1989; Oregon, May 19, 1989; Minnesota, May 22, 1989; Texas, May 25, 1989; Kansas, April 5, 1990; Florida, May 31, 1990; North Dakota, March 25, 1991; Alabama, May 5, 1992; Missouri, May 5, 1992; Michigan, May 7, 1992; New Jersey, May 7, 1992.

Ratification was completed on May 7, 1992.

The amendment was subsequently ratified by Illinois on May 12, 1992 and California on June 26, 1992.

CERTIFICATION OF VALIDITY

Publication of the certifying statement of the Archivist of the United States that the amendment had become valid was made on May 18, 1992, F.R. Doc. 92–11951, 57 F.R. 21187.

[EDITORIAL NOTE: There is some conflict as to the exact dates of ratification of the amendments by the several States. In some cases, the resolutions of ratification were signed by the officers of the legislatures on dates subsequent to that on which the second house had acted. In other cases, the Governors of several of the States "approved" the resolutions (on a subsequent date), although action by the Governor is not contemplated by article V, which required ratification by the legislatures (or conventions) only. In a number of cases, the journals of the State legislatures are not available. The dates set out in this document are based upon the best information available.]

PROPOSED AMENDMENTS TO THE CONSTITUTION NOT RATIFIED BY THE STATES

During the course of our history, in addition to the 27 amendments that have been ratified by the required three-fourths of the States, six other amendments have been submitted to the States but have not been ratified by them.

Beginning with the proposed Eighteenth Amendment, Congress has customarily included a provision requiring ratification within seven years from the time of the submission to the States. The Supreme Court in *Coleman* v. *Miller*, 307 U.S. 433 (1939), declared that the question of the reasonableness of the time within which a sufficient number of States must act is a political question to be determined by the Congress.

In 1789, twelve proposed articles of amendment were submitted to the States. Of these, Articles III–XII were ratified and became the first ten amendments to the Constitution, popularly known as the Bill of Rights. In 1992, proposed Article II was ratified and became the 27th amendment to the Constitution. Proposed Article I which was not ratified is as follows:

"ARTICLE THE FIRST

"After the first enumeration required by the first article of the Constitution, there shall be one Representative for every thirty thousand, until the number shall amount to one hundred, after which the proportion shall be so regulated by Congress, that there shall be not less than one-hundred Representatives, nor less than one Representative for every forty thousand persons, until the number of Representatives shall amount to two hundred; after which the proportion shall be so regulated by Congress, that there shall not be less than two hundred Representatives, nor more than one Representative for every fifty thousand persons."

Thereafter, in the 2d session of the Eleventh Congress, the Congress proposed the following article of amendment to the Constitution relating to acceptance by citizens of the United States of titles of nobility from any foreign government.

The proposed amendment, which was not ratified by three-fourths of the States, is as follows:

Resolved by the Senate and House of Representatives of the United States of America in Congress assembled, two thirds of both houses concurring, That the following section be submitted to the legislatures of the several states, which, when ratified by the legislatures of three fourths of the states, shall be valid and binding, as a part of the constitution of the United States.

If any citizen of the United States shall accept, claim, receive or retain any title of nobility or honour, or shall, without the consent of Congress, accept and retain any present, pension, office or emolument of any kind whatever, from any emperor, king, prince or foreign power, such person shall cease to be a citizen of the United States, and shall be incapable of holding any office of trust or profit under them, or either of them.

The following amendment to the Constitution relating to slavery was proposed by the 2d session of the Thirty-sixth Congress on

March 2, 1861, when it passed the Senate, having previously passed the House on February 28, 1861. It is interesting to note in this connection that this is the only proposed (and not ratified) amendment to the Constitution to have been signed by the President. The President's signature is considered unnecessary because of the constitutional provision that on the concurrence of two-thirds of both Houses of Congress the proposal shall be submitted to the States for ratification.

Resolved by the Senate and House of Representatives of the United States of America in Congress assembled, That the following article be proposed to the Legislatures of the several States as an amendment to the Constitution of the United States, which, when ratified by three-fourths of said Legislatures, shall be valid, to all intents and purposes, as part of the said Constitution, viz:

"ARTICLE THIRTEEN

"No amendment shall be made to the Constitution which will authorize or give to Congress the power to abolish or interfere, within any State, with the domestic institutions thereof, including that of persons held to labor or service by the laws of said State."

A child labor amendment was proposed by the 1st session of the Sixty-eighth Congress on June 2, 1926, when it passed the Senate, having previously passed the House on April 26, 1926. The proposed amendment, which has been ratified by 28 States, to date, is as follows:

JOINT RESOLUTION PROPOSING AN AMENDMENT TO THE CONSTITUTION OF THE UNITED STATES

Resolved by the Senate and House of Representatives of the United States of America in Congress assembled (two-thirds of each House concurring therein), That the following article is proposed as an amendment to the Constitution of the United States, which, when ratified by the legislatures of three-fourths of the several States, shall be valid to all intends and purposes as a part of the Constitution:

"ARTICLE—.

"SECTION 1. The Congress shall have power to limit, regulate, and prohibit the labor of persons under eighteen years of age.

"SECTION 2. The power of the several States is unimpaired by this article except that the operation of State laws shall be suspended to the extent necessary to give effect to legislation enacted by the Congress."

An amendment relative to equal rights for men and women was proposed by the 2d session of the Ninety-second Congress on March 22, 1972, when it passed the Senate, having previously passed the House on October 12, 1971. The seven-year deadline for ratification of the proposed amendment was extended to June 30, 1982, by the 2d session of the Ninety-fifth Congress. The proposed amendment, which was not ratified by three-fourths of the States by June 30, 1982, is as follows:

JOINT RESOLUTION PROPOSING AN AMENDMENT TO THE CONSTITUTION OF THE UNITED STATES RELATIVE TO EQUAL RIGHTS FOR MEN AND WOMEN

Resolved by the Senate and House of Representatives of the United States of America in Congress assembled (two-thirds of each House concurring therein), That the following article is proposed as an amendment to the Constitution of the United States, which shall be valid to all intents and purposes as part of the Constitution when ratified by the legislatures of three-fourths of the several States within seven years from the date of its submission by the Congress:

"ARTICLE—

"SECTION 1. Equality of rights under the law shall not be denied or abridged by the United States or by any State on account of sex.

"SEC. 2. The Congress shall have the power to enforce, by appropriate legislation, the provisions of this article.

"SEC. 3. This amendment shall take effect two years after the date of ratification."

An amendment relative to voting rights for the District of Columbia was proposed by the 2d session of the Ninety-fifth Congress on August 22, 1978, when it passed the Senate, having previously passed the House on March 2, 1978. The proposed amendment, which was not ratified by three-fourths of the States within the specified seven-year period, is as follows:

JOINT RESOLUTION PROPOSING AN AMENDMENT TO THE CONSTITUTION TO PROVIDE FOR REPRESENTATION OF THE DISTRICT OF COLUMBIA IN THE CONGRESS.

Resolved by the Senate and House of Representatives of the United States of America in Congress assembled (two-thirds of each House concurring therein), That the following article is proposed as an amendment to the Constitution of the United States, which shall be valid to all intents and purposes as part of the Constitution when ratified by the legislatures of three-fourths of the several States within seven years from the date of its submission by the Congress:

"ARTICLE—

"SECTION 1. For purposes of representation in the Congress, election of the President and Vice President, and article V of this Constitution, the District constituting the seat of government of the United States shall be treated as though it were a State.

"SEC. 2. The exercise of the rights and powers conferred under this article shall be by the people of the District constituting the seat of government, and as shall be provided by the Congress.

"SEC. 3. The twenty-third article of amendment to the Constitution of the United States is hereby repealed.

"SEC. 4. This article shall be inoperative, unless it shall have been ratified as an amendment to the Constitution by the legislatures of three-fourths of the several States within seven years from the date of its submission."

INDEX TO THE CONSTITUTION AND AMENDMENTS

	Article [1]	Section	Clause
A			
Abridged. The privileges or immunities of citizens of the United States shall not be. [Amendments]	14	1	....
Absent members, in such manner and under such penalties as it may provide. Each House is authorized to compel the attendance of	1	5	1
Accounts of receipts and expenditures of public money shall be published from time to time. A statement of the	1	9	7
Accusation. In all criminal prosecutions the accused shall be informed of the cause and nature of the. [Amendments]	6	....	....
Accused shall have a speedy public trial. In all criminal prosecutions the. [Amendments]	6	....	....
He shall be tried by an impartial jury of the State and district where the crime was committed. [Amendments]	6	....	....
He shall be informed of the nature of the accusation. [Amendments]	6	....	....
He shall be confronted with the witnesses against him. [Amendments]	6	....	....
He shall have compulsory process for obtaining witnesses in his favor. [Amendments]	6	....	....
He shall have the assistance of counsel for his defense. [Amendments]	6	....	....
Actions at common law involving over twenty dollars shall be tried by jury. [Amendments]	7	....	....
Acts, records, and judicial proceedings of another State. Full faith and credit shall be given in each State to the ..	4	1	....
Acts. Congress shall prescribe the manner of proving such acts, records, and proceedings	4	1	....
Adjourn from day to day. A smaller number than a quorum of each House may	1	5	1
Adjourn for more than three days, nor to any other place than that in which they shall be sitting. Neither House shall, during the session of Congress, without the consent of the other	1	5	4
Adjournment, the President may adjourn them to such time as he shall think proper. In case of disagreement between the two Houses as to	2	3	....
Admiralty and maritime jurisdiction. The judicial power shall extend to all cases of	3	2	1
Admitted by the Congress into this Union, but no new States shall be formed or erected within the jurisdiction of any other State. New States may be	4	3	1
Nor shall any State be formed by the junction of two or more States, or parts of States, without the consent of the legislatures and of Congress	4	3	1
Adoption of the Constitution shall be valid. All debts and engagements contracted by the confederation and before the	6	....	1
Advice and consent of the Senate. The President shall have power to make treaties by and with the	2	2	2

[1] Article of original Constitution or of amendment.

INDEX TO THE CONSTITUTION AND AMENDMENTS—Continued

	Article[1]	Section	Clause
To appoint ambassadors or other public ministers and consuls by and with the	2	2	2
To appoint all other officers of the United States not herein otherwise provided for by and with the	2	2	2
Affirmation. Senators sitting to try impeachments shall be on oath or	1	3	6
To be taken by the President of the United States. Form of the oath or	2	1	8
No warrants shall be issued but upon probable cause and on oath or. [Amendments]	4	....	....
To support the Constitution. Senators and Representatives, members of State legislatures, executive and judicial officers, both State and Federal, shall be bound by oath or	6	....	3
Age. No person shall be a Representative who shall not have attained twenty-five years of	1	2	2
No person shall be a Senator who shall not have attained thirty years of	1	3	3
Right of citizens of the United States, who are eighteen years of age or older, to vote shall not be denied or abridged by the United States or any State on account of age. [Amendments]	26	1	....
Agreement or compact with another State without the consent of Congress. No State shall enter into any	1	10	3
Aid and comfort. Treason against the United States shall consist in levying war against them, adhering to their enemies, and giving them	3	3	1
Alliance or confederation. No State shall enter into any treaty of	1	10	1
Ambassadors, or other public ministers and consuls. The President may appoint	2	2	2
The judicial power of the United States shall extend to all cases affecting	3	2	1
Amendments to the Constitution. Whenever two-thirds of both Houses shall deem it necessary, Congress shall propose	5	....	....
On application of the legislatures of two-thirds of the States, Congress shall call a convention to propose ...	5	....	....
Shall be valid when ratified by the legislatures of, or by conventions in, three-fourths of the States	5	....	....
Answer for a capital or infamous crime unless on presentment of a grand jury. No person shall be held to. [Amendments]	5	....	....
Except in cases in the land or naval forces, or in the militia when in actual service. [Amendments]	5	....	....
Appellate jurisdiction both as to law and fact, with such exceptions and under such regulations as Congress shall make. In what cases the Supreme Court shall have	3	2	2
Application of the legislature or the executive of a State. The United States shall protect each State against invasion and domestic violence on the	4	4	....
Application of the legislatures of two-thirds of the States, Congress shall call a convention for proposing amendments to the Constitution. On the	5	....	....
Appointment. Of officers and authority to train the militia reserved to the States respectively	1	8	16
Of such inferior officers as they may think proper in the President alone. Congress may by law vest the ...	2	2	2
In the courts of law or in the heads of departments. Congress may by law vest the	2	2	2
Of Presidential and Vice-Presidential electors. District of Columbia to have power of. [Amendments]	23	1	....

INDEX TO THE CONSTITUTION AND AMENDMENTS—Continued

	Article [1]	Section	Clause
Apportionment of representation and direct taxation among the several States. Provisions relating to the	1	2	3
Congress shall have power to lay and collect taxes on incomes, from whatever source derived, without apportionment among the several States. [Amendments]	16	....	....
Of Representatives among the several States. Provisions relating to the. [Amendments]	14	....	....
Appropriate legislation. Congress shall have power to make all laws necessary and proper for carrying into execution the foregoing powers, and all other powers vested by the Constitution in the Government of the United States, or on any department or officer thereof	1	8	18
Congress shall have power to enforce the thirteenth article, prohibiting slavery by. [Amendments]	13	2	....
Congress shall have power to enforce the provisions of the fourteenth article by. [Amendments]	14	5	....
Congress shall have power to enforce the provisions of the fifteenth article by. [Amendments]	15	2	....
Congress and the several States shall have concurrent power to enforce the provisions of the eighteenth article. [Amendments]	18	2	....
Congress shall have power to enforce the provisions of the nineteenth article. [Amendments]	19	....	....
Congress shall have power to enforce the provisions of the twenty-third article by. [Amendments]	23	2	....
Congress shall have power to enforce the provisions of the twenty-fourth article by. [Amendments]	24	2	....
Congress shall have power to enforce the provisions of the twenty-sixth article by. [Amendments]	26	2	....
Appropriation of money for raising and supporting armies shall be for a longer term than two years. But no	1	8	12
Appropriations made by law. No money shall be drawn from the Treasury but in consequence of	1	9	7
Approve and sign a bill before it shall become a law. The President shall	1	7	2
He shall return it to the House in which it originated with his objections, if he does not	1	7	2
Armies, but no appropriation for that use shall be for a longer term than two years. Congress shall have power to raise and support	1	8	12
Armies. Congress shall make rules for the government and regulation of the land and naval forces	1	8	14
Arms shall not be infringed. A well-regulated militia being necessary to the security of a free State, the right of the people to keep and bear. [Amendments]	2	....	....
Arrest during their attendance at the session of their respective Houses, and in going to and returning from the same. Members shall in all cases, except treason, felony, and breach of the peace, be privileged from	1	6	1
Arsenals. Congress shall exercise exclusive authority over all places purchased for the erection of	1	8	17
Articles exported from any State. No tax or duty shall be laid on	1	9	5
Arts by securing to authors and inventors their patent rights. Congress may promote the progress of science and the useful	1	8	8
Assistance of counsel for his defense. In all criminal prosecutions the accused shall have the. [Amendments]	6	....	....
Assumption of the debt or obligations incurred in aid of rebellion or insurrection against the United States. Provisions against the. [Amendments]	14	4	....

INDEX TO THE CONSTITUTION AND AMENDMENTS—Continued

	Article [1]	Section	Clause
Attainder of treason shall not work corruption of blood or forfeiture, except during the life of the person attainted ..	3	3	2
Attainder or *ex post facto* law shall be passed. No bill of	1	9	3
Attainder, ex post facto law, or law impairing the obligation of contracts. No State shall pass any bill of	1	10	1
Authors and inventors the exclusive right to their writings and inventions. Congress shall have power to secure to ...	1	8	8
B			
Bail. Excessive bail shall not be required, nor excessive fines nor cruel and unusual punishments imposed. [Amendments]	8	....	....
Ballot for President and Vice President. The electors shall vote by. [Amendments]	12	....	....
Ballot. If no person have a majority of the electoral votes for President and Vice President, the House of Representatives shall immediately choose the President by. [Amendments]	12	....	....
Bankruptcies. Congress shall have power to pass uniform laws on the subject of	1	8	4
Basis of representation among the several States. Provisions relating to the. [Amendments]	14	2	....
Bear arms shall not be infringed. A well-regulated militia being necessary to the security of a free State, the right of the people to keep and. [Amendments]	2	....	....
Behavior. The judges of the Supreme and inferior courts shall hold their offices during good	3	1	....
Bill of attainder or *ex post facto* law shall be passed. No	1	9	3
Bill of attainder, *ex post facto* law, or law impairing the obligation of contracts. No State shall pass any	1	10	1
Bills of credit. No State shall emit	1	10	1
Bills for raising revenue shall originate in the House of Representatives. All	1	7	1
Bills which shall have passed the Senate and House of Representatives shall, before they become laws, be presented to the President	1	7	2
If he approve, he shall sign them: if he disapprove, he shall return them, with his objections, to that House in which they originated	1	7	2
Upon the reconsideration of a bill returned by the President with his objections, if two-thirds of each House agree to pass the same, it shall become a law	1	7	2
Upon the reconsideration of a bill returned by the President, the question shall be taken by yeas and nays	1	7	2
Not returned by the President within ten days (Sundays excepted) shall, unless Congress adjourn, become laws	1	7	2
Borrow money on the credit of the United States. Congress shall have power to	1	8	2
Bounties and pensions, shall not be questioned. The validity of the public debt incurred in suppressing insurrection and rebellion against the United States, including the debt for. [Amendments]	14	4	....
Breach of the peace, shall be privileged from arrest while attending the session, and in going to and returning from the same. Senators and Representatives, except for treason, felony, and	1	6	1
Bribery, or other high crimes and misdemeanors. The President, Vice President, and all civil officers shall be removed on impeachment for and conviction of treason ...	2	4	....

INDEX TO THE CONSTITUTION AND AMENDMENTS—Continued

	Article [1]	Section	Clause
C			
Capital or otherwise infamous crime, unless on indictment of a grand jury, except in certain specified cases. No person shall be held to answer for a. [Amendments]	5	....	....
Capitation or other direct tax shall be laid unless in proportion to the census or enumeration. No	1	9	4
Captures on land and water. Congress shall make rules concerning	1	8	11
Casting vote. The Vice President shall have no vote unless the Senate be equally divided	1	3	4
Census or enumeration. Of the inhabitants shall be made within three years after the first meeting of Congress, and within every subsequent term of ten years thereafter	1	2	3
No capitation or other direct tax shall be laid except in proportion to the	1	9	4
Chief Justice shall preside when the President of the United States is tried upon impeachment. The	1	3	6
Choosing the electors and the day on which they shall give their votes, which shall be the same throughout the United States. Congress may determine the time of	2	1	4
Citizen of the United States at the adoption of the Constitution shall be eligible to the office of President. No person not a natural-born	2	1	5
No person shall be a Senator who shall not have attained the age of thirty years, and been nine years a	1	3	3
No person shall be a Representative who shall not have attained the age of twenty-five years, and been seven years a	1	2	2
Right of citizens to vote shall not be denied or abridged by the United States or any State on account of sex. [Amendments]	19	....	....
Right to vote shall not be denied or abridged by the United States or any State for failure to pay any poll tax or other tax. [Amendments]	24	1	....
Right to vote shall not be denied or abridged by the United States or any State to any citizen eighteen years or older, on account of age. [Amendments]	26	1	....
Citizens or subjects of a foreign state. The judicial power of the United States shall not extend to suits in law or equity brought against one of the States by the citizens of another State or by. [Amendments]	11	....	....
Citizenship. Citizens of each State shall be entitled to all the privileges and immunities of citizens of the several States	4	2	1
All persons born or naturalized in the United States, and subject to the jurisdiction thereof, are citizens of the United States and of the State in which they reside. [Amendments]	14	1	....
No State shall make or enforce any law which shall abridge the privileges or immunities of citizens of the United States. [Amendments]	14	1	....
Nor shall any State deprive any person of life, liberty, or property without due process of law. [Amendments]	14	1	....
Nor deny to any person within its jurisdiction the equal protection of the laws. [Amendments]	14	1	....
Civil officers of the United States shall, on impeachment for and conviction of treason, bribery, and other high crimes and misdemeanors be removed. All	2	4	....

INDEX TO THE CONSTITUTION AND AMENDMENTS—Continued

	Article [1]	Section	Clause
Claims of the United States or any particular State in the territory or public property. Nothing in this Constitution shall be construed to prejudice	4	3	2
Classification of Senators. Immediately after they shall be assembled after the first election, they shall be divided as equally as may be into three classes	1	3	2
The seats of the Senators of the first class shall be vacated at the expiration of the second year	1	3	2
The seats of the Senators of the second class at the expiration of the fourth year	1	3	2
The seats of the Senators of the third class at the expiration of the sixth year	1	3	2
Coin a tender in payment of debts. No State shall make anything but gold and silver	1	10	1
Coin money and regulate the value thereof and of foreign coin. Congress shall have power to	1	8	5
Coin of the United States. Congress shall provide for punishing the counterfeiting the securities and current	1	8	6
Color, or previous condition of servitude. The right of citizens of the United States to vote shall not be denied or abridged by the United States or any State on account of race. [Amendments]	15	1	....
Comfort. Treason against the United States shall consist in levying war against them, and giving the enemies aid and	3	3	1
Commander in Chief of the Army and Navy, and of their militia when in actual service. The President shall be	2	2	1
Commerce with foreign nations, among the States, and with Indian tribes. Congress shall have power to regulate	1	8	3
Commerce or revenue. No preference shall be given to the ports of one State over those of another by any regulation of	1	9	6
Vessels clearing from the ports of one State shall not pay duties in those of another	1	9	6
Commissions to expire at the end of the next session. The President may fill vacancies that happen in the recess of the Senate by granting	2	2	3
Common defense, promote the general welfare, &c. To insure the. [Preamble]	....	....	....
Common defense and general welfare. Congress shall have power to provide for the	1	8	1
Common law, where the amount involved exceeds twenty dollars, shall be tried by jury. Suits at. [Amendments]	7	....	....
No fact tried by a jury shall be otherwise reexamined in any court of the United States than according to the rules of the. [Amendments]	7	....	....
Compact with another State. No State shall, without consent of Congress, enter into any agreement or	1	10	3
Compact with a foreign power. No state shall, without the consent of Congress, enter into any agreement or	1	10	3
Compensation of Senators and Representatives to be ascertained by law	1	6	1
Compensation of the President shall not be increased nor diminished during the period for which he shall be elected	2	1	7
Compensation of the judges of the Supreme and inferior courts shall not be diminished during their continuance in office	3	1	....
Compensation. Private property shall not be taken for public use without just. [Amendments]	5	....	....

INDEX TO THE CONSTITUTION AND AMENDMENTS—Continued

	Article [1]	Section	Clause
Compulsory process for obtaining witnesses in his favor. In criminal prosecutions the accused shall have. [Amendments]	6	....	....
Confederation. No State shall enter into any treaty, alliance, or	1	10	1
All debts contracted and engagements entered into before the adoption of this Constitution shall be valid against the United States under it, as under the	6	....	1
Confession in open court. Conviction of treason shall be on the testimony of two persons to the overt act, or upon	3	3	1
Congress of the United States. All legislative powers shall be vested in a	1	1	....
Shall consist of a Senate and House of Representatives	1	1	....
Shall assemble at least once in every year, which shall be on the first Monday of December, unless they by law appoint a different day	1	4	2
May at any time alter regulations for elections of Senators and Representatives, except as to the places of choosing Senators	1	4	1
Each House shall be the judge of the elections, returns, and qualifications of its own members	1	5	1
A majority of each House shall constitute a quorum to do business	1	5	1
A smaller number may adjourn from day to day and compel the attendance of absent members	1	5	1
Each House may determine the rules of its proceedings, punish its members for disorderly behavior, and, with the concurrence of two-thirds, expel a member	1	5	2
Each House shall keep a journal of its proceedings	1	5	3
Neither House, during the session of Congress, shall, without the consent of the other, adjourn for more than three days	1	5	4
Senators and Representatives shall receive a compensation to be ascertained by law	1	6	1
They shall in all cases, except treason, felony, and breach of peace, be privileged from arrest during attendance at their respective Houses, and in going to and returning from the same	1	6	1
No Senator or Representative shall, during his term, be appointed to any civil office which shall have been created, or of which the emoluments shall have been increased, during such term	1	6	2
No person holding any office under the United States, shall, while in office, be a member of either House of Congress	1	6	2
All bills for raising revenue shall originate in the House of Representatives	1	7	1
Proceedings in cases of bills returned by the President with his objections	1	7	2
Shall have power to lay and collect duties, imposts, and excises, pay the debts, and provide for the common defense and general welfare	1	8	1
Shall have power to borrow money on the credit of the United States	1	8	2
To regulate foreign and domestic commerce, and with the Indian tribes	1	8	3
To establish uniform rule of naturalization and uniform laws on the subject of bankruptcies	1	8	4
To coin money, regulate its value and the value of foreign coin, and to fix the standard of weights and measures	1	8	5

INDEX TO THE CONSTITUTION AND AMENDMENTS—Continued

	Article [1]	Section	Clause
To punish counterfeiting of securities and current coin of the United States	1	8	6
To establish post-offices and post-roads	1	8	7
To promote the progress of science and the useful arts	1	8	8
To constitute tribunals inferior to the Supreme Court	1	8	9
To define and punish piracies and felonies on the high seas and to punish offenses against the law of nations	1	8	10
To declare war, grant letters of marque and reprisal, and make rules concerning captures on land and water	1	8	11
To raise and support armies, but no appropriation of money to that use shall be for a longer term than two years	1	8	12
To provide and maintain a Navy	1	8	13
To make rules for the government of the Army and Navy	1	8	14
To call out the militia to execute the laws, suppress insurrections, and repeal invasions	1	8	15
To provide for organizing, arming, and equipping the militia	1	8	16
To exercise exclusive legislation over the District fixed for the seat of government, and over forts, magazines, arsenals, and dockyards	1	8	17
To make all laws necessary and proper to carry into execution all powers vested by the Constitution in the Government of the United States	1	8	18
No person holding any office under the United States shall accept of any present, emolument, office, or title of any kind from any foreign state, without the consent of	1	9	8
May determine the time of choosing the electors for President and Vice President and the day on which they shall give their votes	2	1	4
The President may, on extraordinary occasions, convene either House of	2	3	....
The manner in which the acts, records, and judicial proceedings of the States shall be prescribed by	4	1	....
New States may be admitted by Congress into this Union	4	3	1
Shall have power to make all needful rules and regulations respecting the territory or other property belonging to the United States	4	3	2
Amendments to the Constitution shall be proposed whenever it shall be deemed necessary by two-thirds of both Houses of	5	....	....
Shall have power to enforce, by appropriate legislation, the thirteenth amendment. [Amendments]	13	2	....
Persons engaged in insurrection or rebellion against the United States disqualified for Senators or Representatives in. [Amendments]	14	3	....
But such disqualification may be removed by a vote of two-thirds of both Houses of. [Amendments]	14	3	....
Shall have power to enforce, by appropriate legislation, the fourteenth amendment. [Amendments]	14	5	....
Shall have power to enforce, by appropriate legislation, the fifteenth amendment. [Amendments]	15	2	....
Shall have power to enforce, by appropriate legislation, the nineteenth amendment. [Amendments]	19	....	....
Sessions, time of assembling. [Amendments]	20	2	....

INDEX TO THE CONSTITUTION AND AMENDMENTS—Continued

	Article [1]	Section	Clause
To direct appointment of electors for President and Vice President by District of Columbia. [Amendments]	23	1	....
Shall have power to enforce, by appropriate legislation, the twenty-third amendment. [Amendments]	23	2	....
Shall have power to enforce, by appropriate legislation, the twenty-fourth amendment. [Amendments]	24	2	....
Confirmation by majority vote of Vice President nominated by the President where vacancy in office occurs. [Amendments]	25	2	....
Shall decide the issue of the inability of the President to discharge the powers and duties of his office. [Amendments]	25	4	....
Shall have power to enforce, by appropriate legislation, the twenty-sixth amendment. [Amendments]	26	2	....
No law, varying the compensation for the services of the Senators and Representatives, shall take effect, until an election of Representatives shall have intervened. [Amendments]	27	....	....
Consent. No State shall be deprived of its equal suffrage in the Senate without its	5	....	....
Consent of Congress. No person holding any office of profit or trust under the United States shall accept of any present, emolument, office, or title of any kind whatever, from any king, prince, or foreign potentate, without the ..	1	9	8
No State shall lay any imposts, or duties on imports, except what may be absolutely necessary for executing its inspection laws, without the	1	10	2
No State shall lay any duty of tonnage, keep troops or ships of war in time of peace, without the	1	10	3
No State shall enter into any agreement or compact with another State, or with a foreign power, without the	1	10	3
No State shall engage in war unless actually invaded, or in such imminent danger as will not admit of delay, without the	1	10	3
No new State shall be formed or erected within the jurisdiction of any other State, nor any State be formed by the junction of two or more States, or parts of States, without the consent of the legislatures thereof, as well as the	4	3	1
Consent of the legislature of the State in which the same may be. Congress shall exercise exclusive authority over all places purchased for the erection of forts, magazines, arsenals, dockyards, and other needful buildings by the ..	1	8	17
Consent of the legislatures of the States and of Congress. No States shall be formed by the junction of two or more States or parts of States without the	4	3	1
Consent of the other. Neither House, during the session of Congress, shall adjourn for more than three days, nor to any other place than that in which they shall be sitting, without the	1	5	4
Consent of the owner. No soldier shall be quartered in time of peace in any house without the. [Amendments]	3	....	....
Consent of the Senate. The President shall have power to make treaties, by and with the advice and	2	2	2
The President shall appoint ambassadors, other public ministers and consuls, judges of the Supreme Court, and all other officers created by law and not otherwise herein provided for, by and with the advice and	2	2	2

INDEX TO THE CONSTITUTION AND AMENDMENTS—Continued

	Article [1]	Section	Clause
Constitution, in the Government of the United States, or in any department or officer thereof. Congress shall have power to pass all laws necessary to the execution of the powers vested by the	1	8	18
Constitution, shall be eligible to the office of President. No person except a natural-born citizen, or a citizen at the time of the adoption of the	2	1	5
Constitution. The President, before he enters upon the execution of his office, shall take an oath to preserve, protect, and defend the	2	1	8
Constitution, laws, and treaties of the United States. The judicial power shall extend to all cases arising under the	3	2	1
Constitution shall be so construed as to prejudice any claims of the United States, or of any State (in respect to territory or other property of the United States). Nothing in the	4	3	2
Constitution. The manner in which amendments may be proposed and ratified	5	....	....
Constitution as under the Confederation shall be valid. All debts and engagements contracted before the adoption of the	6	....	1
Constitution and the laws made in pursuance thereof, and all treaties made, or which shall be made, by the United States, shall be the supreme law of the land. The	6	....	2
The judges in every State, anything in the constitution or laws of a State to the contrary notwithstanding, shall be bound thereby	6	....	2
Constitution. All officers, legislative, executive, and judicial, of the United States, and of the several States, shall be bound by an oath to support the	6	....	3
But no religious test shall ever be required as a qualification for any office or public trust	6	....	3
Constitution between the States so ratifying the same. The ratification of the conventions of nine States shall be sufficient for the establishment of the	7	....	....
Constitution, of certain rights, shall not be construed to deny or disparage others retained by the people. The enumeration in the. [Amendments]	9	....	....
Constitution, nor prohibited by it to the States, are reserved to the States respectively or to the people. Powers not delegated to the United States by the. [Amendments]	10	....	....
Constitution, and then engaged in rebellion against the United States. Disqualification for office imposed upon certain class of persons who took an oath to support the. [Amendments]	14	3	....
Constitution. Done in convention by the unanimous consent of the States present, September 17, 1787	7	....	2
Contracts. No State shall pass any ex post facto law, or law impairing the obligation of	1	10	1
Controversies to which the United States shall be a party: between two or more States; between a State and citizens of another State; between citizens of different States; between citizens of the same State claiming lands under grants of different States; between a State or its citizens and foreign states, citizens, or subjects. The judicial power shall extend to	3	2	1
Convene Congress or either House, on extraordinary occasions. The President may	2	3	....
Convention for proposing amendments to the Constitution. Congress, on the application of two-thirds of the legislatures of the States, may call a	5	....	....

INDEX TO THE CONSTITUTION AND AMENDMENTS—Continued

	Article[1]	Section	Clause
Convention, by the unanimous consent of the States present on the 17th of September, 1787. Adoption of the Constitution in	7	....	2
Conventions of nine States shall be sufficient for the establishment of the Constitution. The ratification of the	7	....	....
Conviction in cases of impeachment shall not be had without the concurrence of two-thirds of the members present	1	3	6
Copyrights to authors for limited times. Congress shall have power to provide for	1	8	8
Corruption of blood. Attainder of treason shall not work	3	3	2
Counsel for his defense. In all criminal prosecutions the accused shall have the assistance of. [Amendments]	6	....	....
Counterfeiting the securities and current coin of the United States. Congress shall provide for the punishment of	1	8	6
Courts. Congress shall have power to constitute tribunals inferior to the Supreme Court	1	8	9
Courts as Congress may establish. The judicial power of the United States shall be vested in one Supreme Court and such inferior	3	1	....
Courts. The judges of the Supreme and inferior courts shall hold their offices during good behavior	3	1	....
Their compensation shall not be diminished during their continuance in office	3	1	....
Courts of law. Congress may by law vest the appointment of such inferior officers as they think proper in the President alone, in the heads of departments, or in the	2	2	2
Credit. No State shall emit bills of	1	10	1
Credit of the United States. Congress shall have power to borrow money on the	1	8	2
Credit shall be given in every other State to the public acts, records, and judicial proceedings of each State. Full faith and	4	1	....
Crime, unless on a presentment of a grand jury. No person shall be held to answer for a capital or otherwise infamous. [Amendments]	5	....	....
Except in cases in the military and naval forces, or in the militia when in actual service. [Amendments]	5	....	....
Crimes, except in cases of impeachment, shall be tried by jury. All	3	2	3
They shall be tried in the State within which they may be committed	3	2	3
When not committed in a State, they shall be tried at the places which Congress may by law have provided	3	2	3
Crimes and misdemeanors. The President, Vice President, and all civil officers shall be removed on impeachment for and conviction of treason, bribery, or other	2	4	....
Criminal prosecutions, the accused shall have a speedy and public trial by jury in the State and district where the crime was committed. In all. [Amendments]	6	....	....
He shall be informed of the nature and cause of the accusation. [Amendments]	6	....	....
He shall be confronted with the witnesses against him. [Amendments]	6	....	....
He shall have compulsory process for obtaining witnesses in his favor. [Amendments]	6	....	....
He shall have the assistance of counsel in his defense. [Amendments]	6	....	....
Criminate himself. No person as a witness shall be compelled to. [Amendments]	5	....	....
Cruel and unusual punishments inflicted. Excessive bail shall not be required, nor excessive fines imposed, nor. [Amendments]	8	....	....

INDEX TO THE CONSTITUTION AND AMENDMENTS—Continued

	Article[1]	Section	Clause
D			
Dangers as will not admit of delay. No State shall, without the consent of Congress, engage in war, unless actually invaded, or in such imminent	1	10	3
Day on which they shall vote for President and Vice President, which shall be the same throughout the United States. Congress may determine the time of choosing the electors, and the	2	1	4
Day to day, and may be authorized to compel the attendance of absent members. A smaller number than a quorum of each House may adjourn from	1	5	1
Death, resignation, or inability of the President. In case of, powers and duties of his office shall devolve on the Vice President	2	1	6
[Amendments]	25	....	....
Congress may provide by law for the case of the removal	2	1	6
[Amendments]	25	....	....
Debt of the United States, including debts for pensions and bounties incurred in suppressing insurrection or rebellion, shall not be questioned. The validity of the public. [Amendments]	14	4	....
Debts. No State shall make anything but gold and silver coin a tender in payment of	1	10	1
Debts and provide for the common defense and general welfare of the United States. Congress shall have power to pay the	1	8	1
Debts and engagements contracted before the adoption of this Constitution shall be as valid against the United States, under it, as under the Confederation	6	....	1
Debts or obligations incurred in aid of insurrection or rebellion against the United States, or claims for the loss or emancipation of any slave. Neither the United States nor any State shall assume or pay any. [Amendments]	14	4	....
Declare war, grant letters of marque and reprisal, and make rules concerning captures on land and water. Congress shall have power to	1	8	11
Defense, promote the general welfare, &c. To insure the common. [Preamble]	....	....	....
Defense and general welfare throughout the United States. Congress shall have power to pay the debts and provide for the common	1	8	1
Defense. In all criminal prosecutions the accused shall have the assistance of counsel for his. [Amendments]	6	....	....
Delaware entitled to one Representative in the first Congress	1	2	3
Delay. No State shall, without the consent of Congress, engage in war unless actually invaded, or in such imminent danger as will not admit of	1	10	3
Delegated to the United States, nor prohibited to the States, are reserved to the States or to the people. The powers not. [Amendments]	10	....	....
Deny or disparage others retained by the people. The enumeration in the Constitution of certain rights shall not be construed to. [Amendments]	9	....	....
Departments upon any subject relating to their duties. The President may require the written opinion of the principal officers in each of the executive	2	2	1
Departments. Congress may by law vest the appointment of inferior officers in the heads of	2	2	2

INDEX TO THE CONSTITUTION AND AMENDMENTS—Continued

	Article[1]	Section	Clause
Direct tax shall be laid unless in proportion to the census or enumeration. No capitation or other	1	9	4
Direct taxes and Representatives, how apportioned among the several States	1	2	3
Disability of the President and Vice President. Provisions in case of the	2	1	6
[Amendments]	25	....	....
Disability. No person shall be a Senator or Representative in Congress, or presidential elector, or hold any office, civil or military, under the United States, or any State, who having previously taken an oath as a legislative, executive, or judicial officer of the United States, or of any State, to support the Constitution, afterward engaged in insurrection or rebellion against the United States. [Amendments]	14	3	....
But Congress may, by a vote of two-thirds of each House, remove such. [Amendments]	14	3	....
Disagreement between the two Houses as to the time of adjournment, the President may adjourn them to such time as he may think proper. In case of	2	3	....
Disorderly behavior. Each House may punish its members for	1	5	2
And with the concurrence of two-thirds expel a member	1	5	2
Disparage others retained by the people. The enumeration in the Constitution of certain rights shall not be construed to deny or. [Amendments]	9	....	....
Disqualification. No Senator or Representative shall, during the time for which he was elected, be appointed to any office under the United States which shall have been created or its emoluments increased during such term	1	6	2
No person holding any office under the United States shall be a member of either House during his continuance in office	1	6	2
No person shall be a member of either House, presidential elector, or hold any office under the United States, or any State, who, having previously sworn to support the Constitution, afterward engaged in insurrection or rebellion. [Amendments]	14	3	....
But Congress may, by a vote of two-thirds of each House, remove such disability. [Amendments]	14	3	....
District of Columbia. Congress shall exercise exclusive legislation in all cases over the	1	8	17
Electors for President and Vice President, appointment in such manner as the Congress may direct. [Amendments]	23	1	....
Dockyards. Congress shall have exclusive authority over all places purchased for the erection of	1	8	17
Domestic tranquility, provide for the common defense, &c. To insure. [Preamble]	....	....	....
Domestic violence. The United States shall protect each State against invasion and	4	4	....
Due process of law. No person shall be compelled, in any criminal case, to be a witness against himself, nor be deprived of life, liberty, or property without. [Amendments]	5	....	....
No State shall deprive any person of life, liberty, or property without. [Amendments]	14	1	....
Duties, imposts, and excises. Congress shall have power to lay and collect taxes	1	8	1
Shall be uniform throughout the United States	1	8	1
Duties shall be laid on articles exported from any State. No tax or	1	9	5

INDEX TO THE CONSTITUTION AND AMENDMENTS—Continued

	Article [1]	Section	Clause
Duties in another State. Vessels clearing in the ports of one State shall not be obliged to pay	1	9	6
On imports and exports, without the consent of Congress, except where necessary for executing its inspection laws. No State shall lay any	1	10	2
The net produce of all such duties shall be for the use of the Treasury of the United States	1	10	2
All laws laying such duties shall be subject to the revision and control of Congress	1	10	2
Duties and powers of the office of President, in case of his death, removal, or inability to act, shall devolve on the Vice President	2	1	6
[Amendments]	25	....	....
In case of the disability of the President and Vice President, Congress shall declare what officer shall act	2	1	6
[Amendments]	25	....	....
Duty of tonnage without the consent of Congress. No State shall lay any	1	10	3
E			
Eighteenth Amendment. Repeal. [Amendments]	21	1	....
Election of President and Vice President. Congress may determine the day for the	2	1	4
Shall be the same throughout the United States. The day of the	2	1	4
Elections. The right of citizens of the United States to vote in shall not be denied or abridged by the United States or any State by reason of failure to pay any poll tax or other tax. [Amendments]	24	1	....
Elections for Senators and Representatives. The legislatures of the States shall prescribe the times, places, and manner of holding	1	4	1
But Congress may, at any time, alter such regulations, except as to the places of choosing Senators	1	4	1
Returns and qualifications of its own members. Each House shall be the judge of the	1	5	1
Senators elected by the people. [Amendments]	17	1	....
Electors for members of the House of Representatives. Qualifications of	1	2	1
Electors for Senators. Qualifications of. [Amendments]	17	1	....
Electors for President and Vice President. Each State shall appoint, in such manner as the legislature thereof may direct, a number of electors equal to the whole number of Senators and Representatives to which the State may be entitled in the Congress	2	1	2
But no Senator or Representative, or person holding an office of trust or profit under the United States, shall be appointed an elector	2	1	2
Congress may determine the time of choosing the electors and the day on which they shall give their votes	2	1	4
Which day shall be the same throughout the United States	2	1	4
The electors shall meet in their respective States and vote by ballot for President and Vice President, one of whom, at least, shall not be an inhabitant of the same State with themselves. [Amendments]	12	....	....

INDEX TO THE CONSTITUTION AND AMENDMENTS—Continued

	Article[1]	Section	Clause
The District of Columbia to appoint, in such manner as the Congress may direct, a number of electors equal to the whole number of Senators and Representatives to which the District would be entitled if a State. [Amendments]	23	1	....
Electors shall name, in their ballots, the person voted for as President; and in distinct ballots the person voted for as Vice President. [Amendments]	12	....	....
They shall make distinct lists of the persons voted for as President and of persons voted for as Vice President, which they shall sign and certify, and transmit sealed to the seat of government, directed to the President of the Senate. [Amendments]	12	....	....
No person having taken an oath as a legislative, executive or judicial officer of the United States, or of any State, and afterwards engaged in insurrection or rebellion against the United States, shall be an elector	14	3	....
But Congress may, by a vote of two-thirds of each House, remove such disability. [Amendments]	14	3	....
Emancipation of any slave shall be held to be illegal and void. Claims for the loss or. [Amendments]	14	4	....
Emit bills of credit. No State shall	1	10	1
Emolument of any kind from any king, prince, or foreign state, without the consent of Congress. No person holding any office under the United States shall accept any	1	9	8
Enemies. Treason shall consist in levying war against the United States, in adhering to, or giving aid and comfort to their	3	3	1
Engagements contracted before the adoption of this Constitution shall be valid. All debts and	6	....	1
Enumeration of the inhabitants shall be made within three years after the first meeting of Congress, and within every subsequent term of ten years thereafter	1	2	3
Ratio of representation not to exceed one of every 30,000 until the first enumeration shall be made	1	2	3
Income tax authorized without regard to. [Amendments]	16	....	....
Enumeration in the Constitution of certain rights shall not be construed to deny or disparage others retained by the people. The. [Amendments]	9	....	....
Equal protection of the laws. No State shall deny to any person within its jurisdiction the. [Amendments]	14	1	....
Equal suffrage in the Senate. No State shall be deprived without its consent, of its	5	....	....
Establishment of this Constitution between the States ratifying the same. The ratification of nine States shall be sufficient for the	7	....	....
Ex post facto law shall be passed. No bill of attainder or	1	9	3
Ex post facto law, or law impairing the obligation of contracts. No State shall pass any bill of attainder	1	10	1
Excessive bail shall not be required, nor excessive fines imposed, nor cruel and unusual punishments inflicted. [Amendments]	8	....	....
Excises. Congress shall have power to lay and collect taxes, duties, imposts, and	1	8	1
Shall be uniform throughout the United States. All duties, imposts, and	1	8	1
Exclusive legislation, in all cases, over such district as may become the seat of government. Congress shall exercise	1	8	17
Over all places purchased for the erection of forts, magazines, arsenals, dock-yards and other needful buildings. Congress shall exercise	1	8	17

INDEX TO THE CONSTITUTION AND AMENDMENTS—Continued

	Article [1]	Section	Clause
Executive and judicial officers of the United States and of the several States shall be bound by an oath to support the Constitution	6	....	3
Executive departments. On subjects relating to their duties the President may require the written opinions of the principal officers in each of the	2	2	1
Congress may by law vest the appointment of inferior officers in the heads of	2	2	2
Executive of a State. The United States shall protect each State against invasion and domestic violence, on the application of the legislature or the	4	4	....
Executive power shall be vested in a President of the United States of America. The	2	1	1
Expel a member. Each House, with the concurrence of two-thirds, may	1	5	2
Expenditures of public money shall be published from time to time. A regular statement of the receipts and	1	9	7
Exportations from any State. No tax or duty shall be laid on	1	9	5
Exports or imports, except upon certain conditions. No State shall, without the consent of Congress, lay any duties on	1	10	2
Laid by any State, shall be for the use of the Treasury. The net produce of all duties on	1	10	2
Shall be subject to the revision and control of Congress. All laws of the States laying duties on	1	10	2
Extraordinary occasions. The President may convene both Houses, or either House of Congress, on	2	3	....
F			
Faith and credit in each State shall be given to the acts, records, and judicial proceedings of another State. Full	4	1	....
Felonies committed on the high seas. Congress shall have power to define and punish piracies and	1	8	10
Felony, and breach of the peace. Members of Congress shall not be privileged from arrest for treason	1	6	1
Fines. Excessive fines shall not be imposed. [Amendments]	8	....	....
Foreign coin. Congress shall have power to coin money, fix the standard of weights and measures, and to regulate the value of	1	8	5
Foreign nations, among the States, and with the Indian tribes. Congress shall have power to regulate commerce with	1	8	3
Foreign power. No State shall, without the consent of Congress, enter into any compact or agreement with any	1	10	3
Forfeiture, except during the life of the person attainted. Attainder of treason shall not work	3	3	2
Form of government. The United States shall guarantee to every State in this Union a republican	4	4	....
And shall protect each of them against invasion; and on application of the legislature or of the executive (when the legislature cannot be convened), against domestic violence	4	4	....
Formation of new States. Provisions relating to the	4	3	1
Forts, magazines, arsenals, dock-yards, and other needful buildings. Congress shall exercise exclusive authority over all places purchased for the erection of	1	8	17
Free State, the right of the people to keep and bear arms shall not be infringed. A well-regulated militia being necessary to the security of a. [Amendments]	2	....	....

INDEX TO THE CONSTITUTION AND AMENDMENTS—Continued

	Article [1]	Section	Clause
Freedom of speech or the press. Congress shall make no law abridging the. [Amendments]	1	....	....
Fugitives from crime found in another State shall, on demand, be delivered up to the authorities of the State from which they may flee	4	2	2
Fugitives from service or labor in one State, escaping into another State, shall be delivered up to the party to whom such service or labor may be due	4	2	3
G			
General welfare and secure the blessings of liberty, &c. To promote the. [Preamble.]	....	....	....
General welfare. Congress shall have power to provide for the common defense and	1	8	1
Georgia entitled to three Representatives in the first Congress	1	2	3
Gold and silver coin a tender in payment of debts. No State shall make anything but	1	10	1
Good behavior. The judges of the Supreme and inferior courts shall hold their offices during	3	1	....
Government. The United States shall guarantee to every State in this Union a republican form of	4	4	....
And shall protect each of them against invasion, and on application of the legislature or of the executive (when the legislature cannot be convened) against domestic violence	4	4	....
Grand jury. No person shall be held to answer for a capital or otherwise infamous crime, unless on the presentment of a. [Amendments]	5	....	....
Except in cases arising in the land and naval forces, and in the militia when in actual service. [Amendments]	5	....	....
Guarantee to every State in this Union a republican form of government. The United States shall	4	4	....
And shall protect each of them against invasion; and on application of the legislature or of the executive (when the legislature cannot be convened), against domestic violence	4	4	....
H			
Habeas corpus shall not be suspended unless in cases of rebellion or invasion. The writ of	1	9	2
Heads of departments. Congress may, by law, vest the appointment of inferior officers in the	2	2	2
On any subject relating to their duties, the President may require the written opinion of the principal officers in each of the executive departments	2	2	1
High crimes and misdemeanors. The President, Vice President, and all civil officers shall be removed on impeachment for and conviction of treason, bribery, or other	2	4	....
House of Representatives. Congress shall consist of a Senate and	1	1	....
Shall be composed of members chosen every second year	1	2	1
Qualifications of electors for members of the	1	2	1
No person shall be a member who shall not have attained the age of twenty-five years, and been seven years a citizen of the United States	1	2	2

INDEX TO THE CONSTITUTION AND AMENDMENTS—Continued

	Article [1]	Section	Clause
The executives of the several States shall issue writs of election to fill vacancies in the	1	2	4
Shall choose their Speaker and other officers	1	2	5
Shall have the sole power of impeachment	1	2	5
Shall be the judge of the elections, returns, and qualifications of its own members	1	5	1
A majority shall constitute a quorum to do business	1	5	1
Less than a majority may adjourn from day to day, and compel the attendance of absent members	1	5	1
May determine its own rules of proceedings	1	5	2
May punish its members for disorderly behavior, and, with the concurrence of two-thirds, expel a member	1	5	2
Shall keep a journal of its proceedings	1	5	3
Shall not adjourn for more than three days during the session of Congress without the consent of the Senate	1	5	4
Members shall not be questioned for any speech or debate in either House or in any other place	1	6	1
No person holding any office under the United States shall, while holding such office, be a member of the ..	1	6	2
No person, while a member of either House, shall be appointed to an office which shall have been created or the emoluments increased during his membership	1	6	2
All bills for raising revenue shall originate in the	1	7	1
The votes for President and Vice President shall be counted in the presence of the Senate and. [Amendments]	12	....	....
If no person have a majority of electoral votes, then from the three highest on the list the House of Representatives shall immediately, by ballot, choose a President. [Amendments]	12	....	....
They shall vote by States, each State counting one vote. [Amendments]	12	....	....
A quorum shall consist of a member or members from two-thirds of the States, and a majority of all the States shall be necessary to the choice of a President. [Amendments]	12	....	....
No person having as a legislative, executive, or judicial officer of the United States, or of any State, taken an oath to support the Constitution, and afterwards engaged in insurrection or rebellion against the United States, shall be a member of the. [Amendments]	14	3	....
But Congress may, by a vote of two-thirds of each house, remove such disability. [Amendments]	14	3	....
I			
Imminent danger as will not admit of delay. No State shall, without the consent of Congress, engage in war, unless actually invaded or in such	1	10	3
Immunities. Members of Congress shall, in all cases except treason, felony, and breach of the peace, be privileged from arrest during their attendance at the session of their respective houses, and in going and returning from the same	1	6	1
No soldier shall be quartered in any house without the consent of the owner in time of peace. [Amendments]	3	....	....
No person shall be twice put in jeopardy of life and limb for the same offense. [Amendments]	5	....	....

INDEX TO THE CONSTITUTION AND AMENDMENTS—Continued

	Article [1]	Section	Clause
All persons born or naturalized in the United States, and subject to the jurisdiction thereof, are citizens of the United States and of the State in which they reside. [Amendments]	14	1	....
No State shall make or enforce any law which shall abridge the privileges or immunities of citizens of the United States. [Amendments]	14	1	....
Nor shall any State deprive any person of life, liberty, or property without due process of law. [Amendments]	14	1	....
Nor deny to any person within its jurisdiction the equal protection of the law. [Amendments]	14	1	....
Impeachment. The President may grant reprieves and pardons except in cases of	2	2	1
The House of Representatives shall have the sole power of	1	2	5
Impeachment for and conviction of treason, bribery, and other high crimes and misdemeanors. The President, Vice President, and all civil officers shall be removed upon	2	4	....
Impeachments. The Senate shall have the sole power to try all	1	3	6
The Senate shall be on oath, or affirmation, when sitting for the trial of	1	3	6
When the President of the United States is tried the Chief Justice shall preside	1	3	6
No person shall be convicted without the concurrence of two-thirds of the members present	1	3	6
Judgment shall not extend beyond removal from office and disqualification to hold office	1	3	7
But the party convicted shall be liable to indictment and punishment according to law	1	3	7
Importation of slaves prior to 1808 shall not be prohibited by the Congress	1	9	1
But a tax or duty of ten dollars for each person may be imposed on such	1	9	1
Imports or exports except what may be absolutely necessary for executing its inspection laws. No State shall, without the consent of Congress, lay any imposts or duties on	1	10	2
Imports or exports laid by any State shall be for the use of the Treasury. The net produce of all duties on	1	10	2
Imports or exports shall be subject to the revision and control of Congress. All laws of States laying duties on	1	10	2
Imposts and excises. Congress shall have power to lay and collect taxes, duties	1	8	1
Shall be uniform throughout the United States. All taxes, duties	1	8	1
Inability of the President. The powers and duties of his office shall devolve on the Vice President. In case of the death, resignation, or	2	1	6
[Amendments]	25	....	....
The Vice President shall succeed to the office of the President. In case of the death, resignation, or removal, or [Amendments]	25	....	....
Inability of the President or Vice President. Congress may provide by law for the case of the removal, death, resignation, or	2	1	6
[Amendments]	25	....	....

INDEX TO THE CONSTITUTION AND AMENDMENTS—Continued

	Article[1]	Section	Clause
Income taxes. Congress shall have power to lay and collect without apportionment among the several States, and without regard to any census or enumeration. [Amendments]	16	....	....
Indian tribes. Congress shall have power to regulate commerce with the	1	8	3
Indictment or presentment of a grand jury. No person shall be held to answer for a capital or infamous crime unless on [Amendments]	5	....	....
Except in cases arising in the land and naval forces, and in the militia when in actual service. [Amendments]	5	....	....
Indictment, trial, judgment, and punishment, according to law. The party convicted in case of impeachment shall nevertheless be liable and subject to	1	3	7
Infamous crime unless on presentment or indictment of a grand jury. No person shall be held to answer for a capital or [Amendments]	5	....	....
Inferior courts. Congress shall have power to constitute tribunals inferior to the Supreme Court	1	8	9
Inferior courts as Congress may establish. The judicial power of the United States shall be vested in one Supreme Court and such	3	1	....
The judges of both the Supreme and inferior courts shall hold their offices during good behavior	3	1	....
Their compensation shall not be diminished during their continuance in office	3	1	....
Inferior officers, Congress, if they think proper, may by law vest the appointment of in the President alone, in the courts of law, or in the heads of Departments	2	2	2
Inhabitant of the State for which he shall be chosen. No person shall be a Senator who shall not have attained the age of thirty years, been nine years a citizen of the United States, and who shall not, when elected, be an	1	3	3
Insurrection or rebellion against the United States. No person shall be a Senator or Representative in Congress, or presidential elector, or hold any office, civil or military, under the United States, or any State, who, having taken an oath as a legislative, executive, or judicial officer of the United States, or of a State, afterwards engaged in. [Amendments]	14	3	....
But Congress may, by a vote of two-thirds of each House, remove such disabilities. [Amendments]	14	3	....
Debts declared illegal and void which were contracted in aid of. [Amendments]	14	4	....
Insurrections and repel invasions. Congress shall provide for calling forth the militia to suppress	1	8	15
Intoxicating liquors. Prohibition of manufacture, sale, transportation, importation, or exportation of. [Amendments]	18	1	....
Repeal of Eighteenth Amendment. [Amendments]	21	1	....
Transportation or importation into any State, Territory or possession, for delivery or use therein in violation of their laws, prohibited. [Amendments]	21	2	....
Invasion. No State shall, without the consent of Congress, engage in war unless actually invaded, or in such imminent danger as will not admit of delay	1	10	3
The writ of habeas corpus shall not be suspended unless in case of rebellion or	1	9	2
Invasion and domestic violence. The United States shall protect each State against	4	4	....

INDEX TO THE CONSTITUTION AND AMENDMENTS—Continued

	Article [1]	Section	Clause
Invasions. Congress shall provide for calling forth the militia to suppress insurrections and repel	1	8	15
Inventors and authors in their inventions and writings. Congress may pass laws to secure for limited times exclusive rights to	1	8	8
Involuntary servitude, except as a punishment for crime, abolished in the United States. Slavery and. [Amendments]	13	1	....
J			
Jeopardy of life and limb for the same offense. No person shall be twice put in. [Amendments]	5	....	....
Journal of its proceedings. Each House shall keep a	1	5	3
Judges in every State shall be bound by the Constitution, the laws and treaties of the United States, which shall be the supreme law of the land	6	....	2
Judges of the Supreme and inferior courts shall hold their offices during good behavior	3	1	....
Their compensation shall not be diminished during their continuance in office	3	1	....
Judgment in cases of impeachment shall not extend further than to removal from office, and disqualification to hold any office of honor, trust, or profit under the United States	1	3	7
But the party convicted shall nevertheless be liable and subject to indictment, trial, judgment, and punishment according to law	1	3	7
Judicial and executive officers of the United States and of the several States shall be bound by an oath to support the Constitution	6	....	3
Judicial power of the United States. Congress shall have power to constitute tribunals inferior to the Supreme Court	1	8	9
The judicial power of the United States shall be vested in one Supreme Court, and in such inferior courts as Congress may from time to time ordain and establish	3	1	....
The judges of the Supreme and inferior courts shall hold their offices during good behavior	3	1	....
Their compensation shall not be diminished during their continuance in office	3	1	....
It shall extend to all cases in law and equity arising under the Constitution, laws, and treaties of the United States	3	2	1
To all cases affecting ambassadors, other public ministers, and consuls	3	2	1
To all cases of admiralty and maritime jurisdiction	3	2	1
To controversies to which the United States shall be a party	3	2	1
To controversies between two or more States	3	2	1
To controversies between a State and citizens of another State	3	2	1
[Amendments]	11	....	....
To controversies between citizens of different States	3	2	1
To citizens of the same State claiming lands under grants of different States	3	2	1
To controversies between a State or its citizens and foreign states, citizens, or subjects	3	2	1

INDEX TO THE CONSTITUTION AND AMENDMENTS—Continued

	Article[1]	Section	Clause
In all cases affecting ambassadors, other public ministers and consuls, and those in which a State shall be a party, the Supreme Court shall have original jurisdiction	3	2	2
In all other cases before mentioned, it shall have appellate jurisdiction, both as to law and fact, with such exceptions and under such regulations as Congress shall make	3	2	2
The trial of all crimes, except in cases of impeachment, shall be by jury	3	2	3
The trial shall be held in the State where the crimes shall have been committed	3	2	3
But when not committed in a State, the trial shall be at such place or places as Congress may by law have directed	3	2	3
The judicial power of the United States shall not be held to extend to any suit in law or equity commenced or prosecuted against one of the United States by citizens of another State, or by citizens or subjects of any Foreign State. [Amendments]	11	....	....
Judicial proceedings of every other State. Full faith and credit shall be given in each State to the acts, records, and	4	1	....
Congress shall prescribe the manner of proving such acts, records, and proceedings	4	1	....
Judiciary. The Supreme Court shall have original jurisdiction in all cases affecting ambassadors, other public ministers and consuls, and those in which a State may be a party	3	2	2
The Supreme Court shall have appellate jurisdiction both as to law and fact, with such exceptions and regulations as Congress may make	3	2	2
Junction of two or more States or parts of States without the consent of the legislatures and of Congress. No State shall be formed by the	4	3	1
Jurisdiction of another State. No new State shall, without the consent of Congress, be formed or erected within the	4	3	1
Jurisdiction, both as to law and fact, with such exceptions and under such regulations as Congress may make. The Supreme Court shall have appellate	3	2	2
Jurisdiction. In all cases affecting ambassadors and other public ministers and consuls, and in cases where a State is a party, the Supreme Court shall have original	3	2	2
Jury. The trial of all crimes, except in cases of impeachment, shall be by	3	2	3
In all criminal prosecutions the accused shall have a speedy and public trial by. [Amendments]	6	....	....
All suits at common law, where the value exceeds twenty dollars, shall be tried by. [Amendments]	7	....	....
Where a fact has been tried by a jury it shall not be reexamined except by the rules of the common law. [Amendments]	7	....	....
Just compensation. Private property shall not be taken for public use without. [Amendments]	5	....	....
Justice, insure domestic tranquility, &c. To establish. [Preamble]	....	....	....
L			
Labor, in one State escaping into another State shall be delivered up to the party to whom such service or labor may be due. Fugitives from service or	4	2	3

INDEX TO THE CONSTITUTION AND AMENDMENTS—Continued

	Article [1]	Section	Clause
Land and naval forces. Congress shall make rules for the government and regulation of the	1	8	14
Law and fact, with exceptions and under regulations to be made by Congress. The Supreme Court shall have appellate jurisdiction as to	3	2	2
Law of nations. Congress shall provide for punishing offenses against the	1	8	10
Law of the land. The Constitution, the laws made in pursuance thereof, and treaties of the United States, shall be the supreme	6	....	2
The judges in every State shall be bound thereby	6	....	2
Laws. Congress shall provide for calling forth the militia to suppress insurrection, repel invasion, and to execute the	1	8	15
Laws necessary to carry into execution the powers vested in the government, or in any department or officer of the United States. Congress shall make all	1	8	18
Laws and treaties of the United States. The judicial power shall extend to all cases in law and equity arising under the Constitution, or the	3	2	1
Legal tender in payment of debts. No State shall make anything but gold and silver coin a	1	10	1
Legislation in all cases over such district as may become the seat of government. Congress shall exercise exclusive	1	8	17
Over all places purchased for the erection of forts, magazines, arsenals, dock-yards, and other needful buildings. Congress shall exercise exclusive	1	8	17
Legislation. Congress shall have power to make all laws necessary and proper for carrying into execution all the powers vested by the Constitution in the Government of the United States or in any department or officer thereof	1	8	18
Congress shall have power to enforce the thirteenth amendment, prohibiting slavery, by appropriate. [Amendments]	13	2	....
Congress shall have power to enforce the fourteenth amendment by appropriate. [Amendments]	14	5	....
Congress shall have power to enforce the fifteenth amendment by appropriate. [Amendments]	15	2	....
Congress and the several States shall have concurrent power to enforce the eighteenth amendment by appropriate. [Amendments]	18	2	....
Congress shall have power to enforce the nineteenth amendment by appropriate. [Amendments]	19	....	....
Congress shall have power to enforce the twenty-third amendment by appropriate. [Amendments]	23	2	....
Congress shall have power to enforce the twenty-fourth amendment by appropriate. [Amendments]	24	2	....
Congress shall have power to enforce the twenty-sixth amendment by appropriate. [Amendments]	26	2	....
Legislative powers herein granted shall be vested in Congress. All	1	1	....
Legislature, or the Executive (when the legislature cannot be convened). The United States shall protect each State against invasion and domestic violence, on the application of the	4	4	....
Legislatures of two-thirds of the States, Congress shall call a convention for proposing amendments to the Constitution. On the application of the	5	....	....
Letters of marque and reprisal. Congress shall have power to grant	1	8	11
No State shall grant	1	10	1
Liberty to ourselves and our posterity, &c. To secure the blessings of. [Preamble]	....	....	....

INDEX TO THE CONSTITUTION AND AMENDMENTS—Continued

	Article[1]	Section	Clause
Life or limb for the same offense. No person shall be twice put in jeopardy of. [Amendments]	5	....	....
Life, liberty, and property without due process of law. No person shall be compelled in any criminal case to be a witness against himself, nor be deprived of. [Amendments]	5	....	....
No State shall abridge the privileges or immunities of citizens of the United States, nor deprive any person of. [Amendments]	14	1	....
Loss or emancipation of any slave shall be held illegal and void. Claims for the. [Amendments]	14	4	....
M			
Magazines, arsenals, dock-yards, and other needful buildings. Congress shall have exclusive authority over all places purchased for the erection of	1	8	17
Majority of each House shall constitute a quorum to do business. A	1	5	1
But a smaller number may adjourn from day to day and may be authorized to compel the attendance of absent members	1	5	1
Majority of all the States shall be necessary to a choice. When the choice of a President shall devolve on the House of Representatives, a quorum shall consist of a member or members from two-thirds of the States; but a. [Amendments]	12	....	....
When the choice of a Vice President shall devolve on the Senate, a quorum shall consist of two-thirds of the whole number of Senators, and a majority of the whole number shall be necessary to a choice. [Amendments]	12	....	....
Maritime jurisdiction. The judicial power shall extend to all cases of admiralty and	3	2	1
Marque and reprisal. Congress shall have power to grant letters of	1	8	11
No State shall grant any letters of	1	10	1
Maryland entitled to six Representatives in the first Congress	1	2	3
Massachusetts entitled to eight Representatives in the first Congress	1	2	3
Measures. Congress shall fix the standard of weights and ..	1	8	5
Meeting of Congress. The Congress shall assemble at least once in every year, and such meeting shall be on the first Monday in December, unless they shall by law appoint a different day	1	4	2
Meeting of Electors. The Electors shall meet in their respective States and vote by ballot for President and Vice President, one of whom, at least, shall not be an inhabitant of the same State with themselves. [Amendments]	12	....	....
District of Columbia, electors for President and Vice President appointed by District. [Amendments]	23	1	....
Members of Congress and of State legislatures shall be bound by oath or affirmation to support the Constitution	6	....	3
Militia to execute the laws, suppress insurrections, and repel invasions. Congress shall provide for calling forth the	1	8	15
Congress shall provide for organizing, arming, and disciplining the	1	8	16
Congress shall provide for governing such part of them as may be employed by the United States	1	8	16

INDEX TO THE CONSTITUTION AND AMENDMENTS—Continued

	Article[1]	Section	Clause
Reserving to the States the appointment of the officers and the right to train the militia according to the discipline prescribed by Congress	1	8	16
A well-regulated militia being necessary to the security of a free State, the right of the people to keep and bear arms shall not be infringed. [Amendments]	2	....	....
Misdemeanors. The President, Vice President, and all civil officers shall be removed on impeachment for and conviction of treason, bribery, or other high crimes and	2	4	....
Money on the credit of the United States. Congress shall have power to borrow	1	8	2
Regulate the value thereof and of foreign coin. Congress shall have power to coin	1	8	5
Shall be drawn from the Treasury but in consequence of appropriations made by law. No	1	9	7
Shall be published from time to time. A regular statement and account of receipts and expenditures of public	1	9	7
For raising and supporting armies. No appropriation of money shall be for a longer term than two years	1	8	12
N			
Nations. Congress shall have power to regulate commerce with foreign	1	8	3
Congress shall provide for punishing offenses against the law of	1	8	10
Natural-born citizen, or a citizen at the adoption of the Constitution, shall be eligible for the office of President. No person except a	2	1	5
Naturalization. Congress shall have power to establish a uniform rule of	1	8	4
Naturalized in the United States, and subject to their jurisdiction, shall be citizens of the United States and of the States in which they reside. All persons born, or. [Amendments]	14	1	....
Naval forces. Congress shall make rules and regulations for the government and regulation of the land and	1	8	14
Navy. Congress shall have power to provide and maintain a	1	8	13
New Hampshire entitled to three Representatives in the first Congress	1	2	3
New Jersey entitled to four Representatives in the first Congress	1	2	3
New States may be admitted by Congress into this Union	4	3	1
But no new State shall be formed within the jurisdiction of another State without the consent of Congress	4	3	1
Nor shall any State be formed by the junction of two or more States or parts of States, without the consent of the legislatures and of Congress	4	3	1
New York entitled to six Representatives in the first Congress	1	2	3
Nobility shall be granted by the United States. No title of	1	9	8
No State shall grant any title of	1	10	1
Nominations for office by the President. The President shall nominate, and, by and with the advice and consent of the Senate, shall appoint ambassadors and other public officers	2	2	2
He may grant commissions to fill vacancies that happen in the recess of the Senate, which shall expire at the end of their next session	2	2	3

INDEX TO THE CONSTITUTION AND AMENDMENTS—Continued

	Article [1]	Section	Clause
The President shall nominate a successor to the Vice President whenever a vacancy in office occurs [Amendments]	25	2	....
North Carolina entitled to five Representatives in the first Congress	1	2	3
Number of electors for President and Vice President in each State shall be equal to the number of Senators and Representatives to which such State may be entitled in Congress	2	1	2
O			
Oath of office of the President of the United States. Form of the	2	1	8
Oath or affirmation. No warrants shall be issued but upon probable cause supported by. [Amendments]	4	....	....
Oath or affirmation to support the Constitution. Senators and Representatives, members of State legislatures, executive and judicial officers of the United States and of the several States, shall be bound by	6	....	3
But no religious test shall ever be required as a qualification for office	6	....	3
The Senators when sitting to try impeachment shall be on	1	3	6
Objections. If he shall not approve it, the President shall return the bill to the House in which it originated with his	1	7	2
Obligation of contracts. No State shall pass any ex post facto law, or law impairing the	1	10	1
Obligations incurred in aid of insurrection or rebellion against the United States to be held illegal and void. All debts or. [Amendments]	14	4	....
Offense. No person shall be twice put in jeopardy of life or limb for the same. [Amendments]	5	....	....
Offenses against the law of nations. Congress shall provide for punishing	1	8	10
Against the United States, except in cases of impeachment. The President may grant reprieves or pardons for	2	2	1
Office under the United States. No person shall be a member of either House while holding any civil	1	6	2
No Senator or Representative shall be appointed to any office under the United States which shall have been created, or its emoluments increased, during the term for which he is elected	1	6	2
Or title of any kind from any king, prince, or foreign State, without the consent of Congress. No person holding any office under the United States shall accept any present, emolument	1	9	8
Office of President, in case of his removal, death, resignation, or inability, shall devolve on the Vice President. The powers and duties of the	2	1	6
[Amendments]	25	....	....
During the term of four years. The President and Vice President shall hold	2	1	1
Of trust or profit under the United States shall be an elector for President and Vice President. No person holding an	2	1	2

INDEX TO THE CONSTITUTION AND AMENDMENTS—Continued

	Article[1]	Section	Clause
Civil or military under the United States, or any State, who had taken an oath as a legislative, executive, or judicial officer of the United States, or of any State, and afterward engaged in insurrection or rebellion. No person shall be a Senator, Representative or President elector, or hold any. [Amendments]	14	3	....
Officers in the President alone, in the courts of law, or in the heads of Departments. Congress may vest the appointment of inferior	2	2	2
Of the United States shall be removed on impeachment for and conviction of treason, bribery, or other high crimes and misdemeanors. The President, Vice President, and all civil	2	4	....
The House of Representatives shall choose their Speaker and other	1	2	5
The Senate, in the absence of the Vice President, shall choose a President *pro tempore,* and also their other	1	3	5
Offices becoming vacant in the recess of the Senate may be filled by the President, the commissions to expire at the end of the next session	2	2	3
One-fifth of the members present, be entered on the journal of each House. The yeas and nays shall, at the desire of	1	5	3
Opinion of the principal officers in each of the Executive Departments on any subject relating to their duties. The President may require the written	2	2	1
Order, resolution, or vote (except on a question of adjournment) requiring the concurrence of the two Houses, shall be presented to the President. Every	1	7	3
Original jurisdiction, in all cases affecting ambassadors, other public ministers, and consuls, and in which a State may be a party. The Supreme Court shall have	3	2	2
Overt act, or on confession in open court. Conviction of treason shall be on the testimony of two witnesses to the	3	3	1
P			
Pardons, except in cases of impeachment. The President may grant reprieves and	2	2	1
Patent rights to inventors. Congress may pass laws for securing	1	8	8
Peace. Members of Congress shall not be privileged from arrest for treason, felony, and breach of the	1	6	1
No State shall, without the consent of Congress, keep troops or ships of war in time of	1	10	3
No soldier shall be quartered in any house without the consent of the owner in time of. [Amendments]	3	....	....
Pennsylvania entitled to eight Representatives in the first Congress	1	2	3
Pensions and bounties shall not be questioned. The validity of the public debt incurred in suppressing insurrection and rebellion against the United States, including the debt for. [Amendments]	14	4	....
People, peaceably to assemble and petition for redress of grievances, shall not be abridged by Congress. The right of the. [Amendments]	1	....	....
To keep and bear arms shall not be infringed. A well-regulated militia being necessary to the security of a free State, the right of the. [Amendments]	2	....	....
To be secure in their persons, houses, papers, and effects, against unreasonable searches and seizures shall not be violated. The right of the. [Amendments]	4	....	....

INDEX TO THE CONSTITUTION AND AMENDMENTS—Continued

	Article [1]	Section	Clause
People. The enumeration of certain rights in the Constitution shall not be held to deny or disparage others retained by the. [Amendments]	9	....	....
Powers not delegated to the United States, nor prohibited to the States, are reserved to the States or to the. [Amendments]	10	....	....
Perfect Union, &c. To establish a more. [Preamble]	....	....	....
Persons, houses, papers, and effects against unreasonable searches and seizures. The people shall be secure in their. [Amendments]	4	....	....
Persons, as any State may think proper to admit, shall not be prohibited prior to 1808. The migration or importation of such	1	9	1
But a tax or duty of ten dollars shall be imposed on the importation of each of such	1	9	1
Petition for the redress of grievances. Congress shall make no law abridging the right of the people peaceably to assemble and to. [Amendments]	1	....	....
Piracies and felonies committed on the high seas. Congress shall define and punish	1	8	10
Place than that in which the two Houses shall be sitting. Neither House during the session shall, without the consent of the other, adjourn for more than three days, nor to any other	1	5	4
Places of choosing Senators. Congress may by law make or alter regulations for the election of Senators and Representatives, except as to the	1	4	1
Poll tax. The right of citizens of the United States to vote shall not be denied or abridged by the United States or any State by reason of failure to pay. [Amendments]	24	1	....
Ports of one State over those of another. Preference shall not be given by any regulation of commerce or revenue to the	1	9	6
Vessels clearing from the ports of one State shall not pay duties in another	1	9	6
Post offices and post roads. Congress shall establish	1	8	7
Powers herein granted shall be vested in Congress. All legislative	1	1	....
Powers vested by the Constitution in the Government or in any Department or officer of the United States. Congress shall make all laws necessary to carry into execution the	1	8	18
Powers and duties of the office shall devolve on the Vice President, on the removal, death, resignation, or inability of the President. The	2	1	6
[Amendments]	25	....	....
Powers not delegated to the United States nor prohibited to the States are reserved to the States and to the people. [Amendments]	10	....	....
The enumeration of certain rights in this Constitution shall not be held to deny or disparage others retained by the people. [Amendments]	9	....	....
Preference, by any regulation of commerce or revenue, shall not be given to the ports of one State over those of another	1	9	6
Prejudice any claims of the United States or of any particular State in the territory or property of the United States. Nothing in this Constitution shall	4	3	2
Present, emolument, office, or title of any kind whatever from any king, prince, or foreign State. No person holding any office under the United States shall, without the consent of Congress, accept any	1	9	8

INDEX TO THE CONSTITUTION AND AMENDMENTS—Continued

	Article [1]	Section	Clause
Presentment or indictment of a grand jury, except in cases arising in the land or naval forces, or in the militia when in actual service. No person shall be held to answer for a capital or otherwise infamous crime unless on a. [Amendments]	5	....	....
President of the United States. The Senate shall choose a President *pro tempore* when the Vice President shall exercise the office of	1	3	5
Additional provision for succession through act of Congress. [Amendments]	20	4	....
Succession in case of death. [Amendments]	20	3	....
Succession in case of failure to be chosen or qualified. [Amendments]	20	3	....
Term of office, beginning and ending. [Amendments]	20	1	....
The Chief Justice shall preside upon the trial of the	1	3	6
Shall approve and sign all bills passed by Congress before they shall become laws	1	7	2
Shall return to the House in which it originated, with his objections, any bill which he shall not approve	1	7	2
If not returned within ten days (Sundays excepted), it shall become a law, unless Congress shall adjourn before the expiration of that time	1	7	2
Every order, resolution, or vote which requires the concurrence of both Houses, except on a question of adjournment, shall be presented to the	1	7	3
If disapproved by him, shall be returned and proceeded on as in the case of a bill	1	7	3
The executive power shall be vested in a	2	1	1
He shall hold his office during the term of four years	2	1	1
In case of the removal of the President from office, or of his death, resignation, or inability to discharge the duties of his office, the Vice President shall perform the duties of	2	1	6
[Amendments]	25	....	....
Congress may declare, by law, in the case of the removal, death, resignation, or inability of the President, what officer shall act as	2	1	6
[Amendments]	25	....	....
The President shall receive a compensation which shall not be increased nor diminished during his term, nor shall he receive any other emolument from the United States	2	1	7
Before he enters upon the execution of his office he shall take an oath of office	2	1	8
Shall be Commander in Chief of the Army and Navy and of the militia of the States when called into actual service	2	2	1
He may require the opinion, in writing, of the principal officer in each of the Executive Departments	2	2	1
He may grant reprieves or pardons for offenses, except in cases of impeachment	2	2	1
He may make treaties by and with the advice and consent of the Senate, two-thirds of the Senators present concurring	2	2	2
He may appoint, by and with the advice and consent of the Senate, ambassadors, other public ministers and consuls, judges of the Supreme Court, and all other officers whose appointments may be authorized by law and not herein provided for	2	2	2
Congress may vest the appointment of inferior officers in the	2	2	2

INDEX TO THE CONSTITUTION AND AMENDMENTS—Continued

	Article [1]	Section	Clause
He may fill up all vacancies that may happen in the recess of the Senate by commissions which shall expire at the end of their next session	2	2	3
He shall give information to Congress of the state of the Union, and recommend measures	2	3	....
On extraordinary occasions he may convene both Houses or either	2	3	....
In case of disagreement between the two Houses as to the time of adjournment, he may adjourn them to such time as he may think proper	2	3	....
He shall receive ambassadors and other public ministers	2	3	....
He shall take care that the laws be faithfully executed	2	3	....
He shall commission all the officers of the United States	2	3	....
On impeachment for, and conviction of, treason, bribery, or other high crimes and misdemeanors, shall be removed from office. The	2	4	....
No person except a natural-born citizen, or a citizen of the United States at the adoption of the Constitution, shall be eligible to the office of	2	1	5
No person shall be elected to office more than twice. [Amendments]	22	....	....
No person who shall not have attained the age of thirty-five years and been fourteen years a resident of the United States shall be eligible for the office of	2	1	5
Congress to decide the issue of the President's ability to discharge the powers and duties of his office. [Amendments]	25	4	....
Declaration of his inability to discharge the powers and duties of his office. [Amendments]	25	3	....
Nomination of successor to the Vice President whenever a vacancy in the office of the Vice President occurs. [Amendments]	25	2	....
Succession of Vice President to office in case of death, resignation, removal, or inability of President to discharge the powers and duties of his office. [Amendments]	25	....	....
President and Vice President. Manner of choosing. Each State by its legislature, shall appoint a number of electors equal to the whole number of Senators and Representatives to which the State may be entitled in the Congress	2	1	2
No Senator or Representative or person holding an office of trust or profit under the United States shall be an elector	2	1	2
Congress may determine the time of choosing the electors and the day on which they shall give their votes, which day shall be the same throughout the United States	2	1	4
The electors shall meet in their respective States and vote by ballot for President and Vice President, one of whom, at least, shall not be an inhabitant of the same State with themselves. [Amendments]	12	....	....
They shall name in distinct ballots the person voted for as President and the person voted for as Vice President. [Amendments]	12	....	....

INDEX TO THE CONSTITUTION AND AMENDMENTS—Continued

	Article [1]	Section	Clause
They shall make distinct lists of the persons voted for as President and as Vice President, which they shall sign and certify and transmit sealed to the President of the Senate at the seat of government. [Amendments]	12	....	....
The President of the Senate shall, in the presence of the Senate and House of Representatives, open all the certificates, and the votes shall then be counted. [Amendments]	12	....	....
The person having the greatest number of votes shall be the President, if such number be a majority of the whole number of electors appointed. [Amendments]	12	....	....
If no person have such majority, then from the persons having the highest numbers, not exceeding three, on the list of those voted for as President, the House of Representatives shall choose immediately, by ballot, the President. [Amendments]	12	....	....
In choosing the President, the votes shall be taken by States, the representation from each State having one vote. [Amendments]	12	....	....
A quorum for this purpose shall consist of a member or members from two-thirds of the States, and a majority of all the States shall be necessary to a choice. [Amendments]	12	....	....
But if no choice shall be made before the 4th of March next following, then the Vice President shall act as President, as in the case of the death or disability of the President. [Amendments]	12	....	....
The District of Columbia shall appoint, in such manner as the Congress may direct, a number of electors equal to the whole number of Senators and Representatives to which the District would be entitled if a State. [Amendments]	23	1	....
President of the Senate, but shall have no vote unless the Senate be equally divided. The Vice President shall be	1	3	4
President pro tempore. In the absence of the Vice President the Senate shall choose a	1	3	5
When the Vice President shall exercise the office of President of the United States, the Senate shall choose a	1	3	5
President to transmit his declaration of inability to discharge the powers and duties of his office to. [Amendments]	25	3	....
Vice President and a majority of the principal officers of the executive departments to transmit their declaration of the President's inability to discharge the powers and duties of his office to. [Amendments]	25	4	....
Press. Congress shall pass no law abridging the freedom of speech or of the. [Amendments]	1	....	....
Previous condition of servitude. The right of citizens of the United States to vote shall not be denied or abridged by the United States, or by any State, on account of race, color, or. [Amendments]	15	1	....
Primary elections. The right of citizens of the United States to vote in shall not be denied or abridged by the United States or any State by reason of failure to pay any poll tax or other tax. [Amendments]	24	1	....
Private property shall not be taken for public use without just compensation. [Amendments]	5	....	....

INDEX TO THE CONSTITUTION AND AMENDMENTS—Continued

	Article [1]	Section	Clause
Privilege. Senators and Representatives shall, in all cases except treason, felony, and breach of the peace, be privileged from arrest during their attendance at the session of their respective Houses, and in going to and returning from the same	1	6	1
They shall not be questioned for any speech or debate in either House in any other place	1	6	1
Privileges and immunities of citizens of the United States. The citizens of each State shall be entitled to all the privileges and immunities of the citizens of the several States	4	2	1
No soldier shall be quartered in any house without the consent of the owner in time of peace. [Amendments]	3	....	....
No person shall be twice put in jeopardy of life and limb for the same offense. [Amendments]	5	....	....
All persons born or naturalized in the United States, and subject to the jurisdiction thereof, are citizens of the United States and of the State in which they reside. [Amendments]	14	1	....
No State shall make or enforce any law which shall abridge the privileges or immunities of citizens of the United States. [Amendments]	14	1	....
No State shall deprive any person of life, liberty, or property without due process of law. [Amendments]	14	1	....
Nor deny to any person within its jurisdiction the equal protection of its laws. [Amendments]	14	1	....
Prizes captured on land or water. Congress shall make rules concerning	1	8	11
Probable cause. The right of the people to be secure in their persons, houses, papers, and effects, against unreasonable searches and seizures, shall not be violated. And no warrant shall issue for such but upon. [Amendments]	4	....	....
Process for obtaining witnesses in his favor. In all criminal prosecutions the accused shall have. [Amendments]	6	....	....
Process of law. No person shall be compelled in any criminal case to be a witness against himself, nor be deprived of life, liberty, or property, without due. [Amendments]	5	....	....
No State shall deprive any person of life, liberty, or property, without due. [Amendments]	14	1	....
Progress of science and useful arts. Congress shall have power to promote the	1	8	8
Property of the United States. Congress may dispose of and make all needful rules and regulations respecting the territory or	4	3	3
Property, without due process of law. No person shall be compelled in any criminal case to be a witness against himself; nor shall he be deprived of his life, liberty, or. [Amendments]	5	....	....
No State shall abridge the privileges or immunities of citizens of the United States; nor deprive any person of his life, liberty, or. [Amendments]	14	1	....
Prosecutions. The accused shall have a speedy and public trial in all criminal. [Amendments]	6	....	....
He shall be tried by a jury in the State or district where the crime was committed. [Amendments]	6	....	....
He shall be informed of the nature and cause of the accusation. [Amendments]	6	....	....
He shall be confronted with the witnesses against him. [Amendments]	6	....	....
He shall have compulsory process for obtaining witnesses. [Amendments]	6	....	....
He shall have counsel for his defense. [Amendments]	6	....	....

INDEX TO THE CONSTITUTION AND AMENDMENTS—Continued

	Article[1]	Section	Clause
Protection of the laws. No State shall deny to any person within its jurisdiction the equal. [Amendments]	14	1	....
Public debt of the United States incurred in suppressing insurrection or rebellion shall not be questioned. The validity of the. [Amendments]	14	4	....
Public safety must require it. The writ of *habeas corpus* shall not be suspended, unless when in cases of rebellion or invasion the	1	9	2
Public trial by jury. In all criminal prosecutions the accused shall have a speedy and. [Amendments]	6	....	....
Public use. Private property shall not be taken for, without just compensation. [Amendments]	5	....	....
Punishment according to law. Judgment in cases of impeachment shall not extend further than to removal from, and disqualification for, office; but the party convicted shall nevertheless be liable and subject to indictment, trial, judgment, and	1	3	7
Punishments inflicted. Excessive bail shall not be required nor excessive fines imposed nor cruel and unusual. [Amendments]	8	....	....
Q			
Qualification for office. No religious test shall ever be required as a	6	....	3
Qualifications of electors of members of the House of Representatives shall be the same as electors for the most numerous branch of the State legislature	1	2	1
Qualifications of electors of Senators shall be the same as electors of the most numerous branch of the State legislature. [Amendments]	17	1	....
Qualifications of members of the House of Representatives. They shall be twenty-five years of age, seven years a citizen of the United States, and an inhabitant of the State in which chosen	1	2	2
Of Senators. They shall be thirty years of age, nine years a citizen of the United States, and an inhabitant of the State in which chosen	1	3	3
Of its own members. Each House shall be the judge of the election, returns, and	1	5	1
Of the President. No person except a natural-born citizen, or a citizen of the United States at the time of the adoption of the Constitution, shall be eligible to the office of President	2	1	5
Neither shall any person be eligible to the office of President who shall not have attained the age of thirty-five years and been fourteen years a resident within the United States	2	1	5
Of the Vice President. No person constitutionally ineligible to the office of President shall be eligible to that of Vice President. [Amendments]	12	....	....
Quartered in any house without the consent of the owner in time of peace. No soldier shall be. [Amendments]	3	....	....
Quorum to do business. A majority of each House shall constitute a	1	5	1
But a smaller number than a quorum may adjourn from day to day and may be authorized to compel the attendance of absent members	1	5	1
Of the House of Representatives for choosing a President shall consist of a member or members from two-thirds of the States, and a majority of all the States shall be necessary to a choice. [Amendments]	12	....	....

INDEX TO THE CONSTITUTION AND AMENDMENTS—Continued

	Article [1]	Section	Clause
Quorum to elect a Vice President by the Senate. Two-thirds of the whole number of Senators shall be a. [Amendments]	12	....	....
A majority of the whole number shall be necessary to a choice. [Amendments]	12	....	....
R			
Race, color, or previous condition of servitude. The right of citizens of the United States to vote shall not be denied or abridged by the United States or by any State on account of. [Amendments]	15	1	....
Ratification of amendments to the Constitution shall be by the legislatures of three-fourths of the several States or by conventions in three-fourths of the States, accordingly as Congress may propose	5	....	....
Ratification of the conventions of nine States shall be sufficient to establish the Constitution between the States so ratifying the same	7	....	....
Ratio of representation until the first enumeration under the Constitution shall be made not to exceed one for every thirty thousand	1	2	3
Ratio of representation shall be apportioned among the several States according to their respective numbers, counting the whole number of persons in each State, excluding Indians not taxed. [Amendments]	14	2	....
But when the right to vote for Presidential electors or members of Congress, or the legislative, executive, and judicial officers of the State, except for engaging in rebellion or other crime, shall be denied or abridged by a State, the basis of representation shall be reduced therein in the proportion of such denial or abridgment of the right to vote. [Amendments]	14	2	....
Rebellion against the United States. Persons who, while holding certain Federal and State offices, took an oath to support the Constitution, afterward engaged in insurrection or rebellion, disabled from holding office under the United States. [Amendments]	14	3	....
But Congress may by a vote of two-thirds of each House remove such disability. [Amendments]	14	3	....
Debts incurred for pensions and bounties for services in suppressing the rebellion shall not be questioned. [Amendments]	14	4	....
All debts and obligations incurred in aid of the rebellion, and all claims for the loss or emancipation of slaves, declared and held to be illegal and void. [Amendments]	14	4	....
Rebellion or invasion. The writ of habeas corpus shall not be suspended except when the public safety may require it in cases of	1	9	2
Receipts and expenditures of all public money shall be published from time to time. A regular statement of	1	9	7
Recess of the Senate. The President may grant commissions, which shall expire at the end of the next session, to fill vacancies that may happen during the	2	2	3
Reconsideration of a bill returned by the President with his objections. Proceedings to be had upon the	1	7	2
Records, and judicial proceedings of every other State. Full faith and credit shall be given in each State to the acts	4	1	....
Congress shall prescribe the manner of proving such acts, records, and proceedings	4	1	....

INDEX TO THE CONSTITUTION AND AMENDMENTS—Continued

	Article [1]	Section	Clause
Redress of grievances. Congress shall make no law abridging the right of the people peaceably to assemble and to petition for the. [Amendments]	1	....	....
Regulations, except as to the places of choosing Senators. The time, places, and manner of holding elections for Senators and Representatives shall be prescribed by the legislatures of the States, but Congress may at any time by law make or alter such	1	4	1
Regulations of commerce or revenue. Preference to the ports of one State over those of another shall not be given by any	1	9	6
Religion or prohibiting the free exercise thereof. Congress shall make no law respecting the establishment of. [Amendments]	1	....	....
Religious test shall ever be required as a qualification for any office or public trust under the United States. No	6	....	3
Removal of the President from office. The same shall devolve on the Vice President. In case of the	2	1	6
[Amendments]	25	....	....
The Vice President shall succeed to the office of the President. In case of the death, resignation, inability, or. [Amendments]	25	....	....
Representation. No State, without its consent, shall be deprived of its equal suffrage in the Senate	5	....	....
Representation and direct taxation, how apportioned among the several States	1	2	3
Representation until the first enumeration under the Constitution not to exceed one for every thirty thousand. The ratio of	1	2	3
Representation in any State. The executive thereof shall issue writs of election to fill vacancies in the	1	2	4
Representation among the several States shall be according to their respective numbers, counting the whole number of persons in each State, excluding Indians not taxed. The ratio of. [Amendments]	14	2	....
But where the right to vote in certain Federal and State elections is abridged for any cause other than rebellion or other crime, the basis of representation shall be reduced. [Amendments]	14	2	....
Representatives. Congress shall consist of a Senate and House of	1	1	....
Qualifications of electors of members of the House of	1	2	1
No person shall be a Representative who shall not have attained the age of twenty-five years, been seven years a citizen of the United States, and an inhabitant of the State in which he shall be chosen	1	2	2
And direct taxes, how apportioned among the several States	1	2	3
Executives of the State shall issue writs of election to fill vacancies in the House of	1	2	4
Shall choose their Speaker and other officers. The House of	1	2	5
Shall have the sole power of impeachment. The House of	1	2	5
The times, places, and manner of choosing Representatives shall be prescribed by the legislatures of the States	1	4	1
But Congress may make by law at any time or alter such regulations except as to the places of choosing Senators	1	4	1
And Senators shall receive a compensation, to be ascertained by law	1	6	1

INDEX TO THE CONSTITUTION AND AMENDMENTS—Continued

	Article[1]	Section	Clause
Shall in all cases, except treason, felony, and breach of the peace, be privileged from arrest during attendance at the session of the House, and in going to and returning from the same	1	6	1
Shall not be questioned in any other place for any speech or debate. Members of the House of	1	6	1
No member shall be appointed during his term to any civil office which shall have been created, or the emoluments of which shall have been increased, during such term	1	6	2
No person holding any office under the United States shall, while holding such office, be a member of the House of	1	6	2
All bills for raising revenue shall originate in the House of	1	7	1
No Senator or Representative shall be an elector for President or Vice President	2	1	2
No law, varying the compensation for the services of the Senators and Representatives, shall take effect, until an election of Representatives shall have intervened. [Amendments]	27	....	....
Representatives shall be bound by an oath or affirmation to support the Constitution of the United States. The Senators and	6	....	3
Representatives among the several States. Provisions relative to the apportionment of. [Amendments]	14	2	....
Representatives and Senators. Prescribing certain disqualifications for office as. [Amendments]	14	3	....
But Congress may, by a vote of two-thirds of each House, remove such disqualification. [Amendments]	14	3	....
Reprieves and pardons except in cases of impeachment. The President may grant	2	2	1
Reprisal. Congress shall have power to grant letters of marque and	1	8	11
No State shall grant any letters of marque and	1	10	1
Republican form of government. The United States shall guarantee to every State in this Union a	4	4	....
And shall protect each of them against invasion; and on the application of the legislature, or of the executive (when the legislature cannot be convened), against domestic violence	4	4	....
Reserved rights of the States and the people. The enumeration in the Constitution of certain rights shall not be construed to deny or disparage others retained by the people. [Amendments]	9	....	....
The powers not delegated to the United States by the Constitution, nor prohibited by it to the States, are reserved to the States respectively, or to the people. [Amendments]	10	....	....
Resignation of the President. The duties and powers of his office shall devolve on the Vice President. In case of the death	2	1	6
Congress may by law provide for the case of the removal, death	2	1	6
The Vice President shall succeed to the office of the President. In case of the death, removal, inability, or [Amendments]	25	....	....
Resolution, or vote (except on a question of adjournment) requiring the concurrence of the two Houses shall, before it becomes a law, be presented to the President. Every order	1	7	3

INDEX TO THE CONSTITUTION AND AMENDMENTS—Continued

	Article [1]	Section	Clause
Revenue shall originate in the House of Representatives. All bills for raising	1	7	1
Revenue. Preference shall not be given to the ports of one State over those of another by any regulations of commerce or	1	9	6
Rhode Island entitled to one Representative in the first Congress	1	2	3
Right of petition. Congress shall make no law abridging the right of the people peaceably to assemble and to petition for the redress of grievances. [Amendments]	1	....	....
Right to keep and bear arms. A well-regulated militia being necessary to the security of a free State, the right of the people to keep and bear arms shall not be infringed. [Amendments]	2	....	....
Rights in the Constitution shall not be construed to deny or disparage others retained by the people. The enumeration of certain. [Amendments]	9	....	....
Rights not delegated to the United States nor prohibited to the States are reserved to the States or to the people. [Amendments]	10	....	....
Rules of its proceedings. Each House may determine the	1	5	2
Rules and regulations respecting the territory or other property of the United States. Congress shall dispose of and make all needful	4	3	2
Rules of the common law. All suits involving over twenty dollars shall be tried by jury according to the. [Amendments]	7	....	....
No fact tried by a jury shall be re-examined except according to the. [Amendments]	7	....	....
S			
Science and the useful arts by securing to authors and inventors the exclusive right to their writings and discoveries. Congress shall have power to promote the progress of	1	8	8
Searches and seizures shall not be violated. The right of the people to be secure against unreasonable. [Amendments]	4	....	....
And no warrants shall be issued but upon probable cause, on oath or affirmation, describing the place to be searched and the persons or things to be seized. [Amendments]	4	....	....
Seat of Government. Congress shall exercise exclusive legislation in all cases over such district as may become the	1	8	17
Securities and current coin of the United States. Congress shall provide for punishing the counterfeiting of the	1	8	6
Security of a free State, the right of the people to keep and bear arms shall not be infringed. A well-regulated militia being necessary to the. [Amendments]	2	....	....
Senate and House of Representatives. The Congress of the United States shall consist of a	1	1	....
Senate of the United States. The Senate shall be composed of two Senators from each State, chosen by the legislature for six years	1	3	1
The Senate shall be composed of two Senators from each State, elected by the people thereof, for six years. [Amendments]	17	1	....
Qualifications of electors of Senators. [Amendments]	17	1	....

INDEX TO THE CONSTITUTION AND AMENDMENTS—Continued

	Article[1]	Section	Clause
If vacancies happen during the recess of the legislature of a State, the executive thereof may make temporary appointments until the next meeting of the legislature	1	3	2
When vacancies happen the executive authority of the State shall issue writs of election to fill such vacancies; provided, that the legislature of any State may empower the executive thereof to make temporary appointment until the people fill the vacancies by election as the legislature may direct. [Amendments]	17	2	....
The Vice President shall be President of the Senate, but shall have no vote unless the Senate be equally divided	1	3	4
The Senate shall choose their other officers, and also a President *pro tempore* in the absence of the Vice President or when he shall exercise the office of President	1	3	5
The Senate shall have the sole power to try all impeachments. When sitting for that purpose they shall be on oath or affirmation	1	3	6
When the President of the United States is tried the Chief Justice shall preside; and no person shall be convicted without the concurrence of two-thirds of the members present	1	3	6
It shall be the judge of the elections, returns, and qualifications of its own members	1	5	1
A majority shall constitute a quorum to do business, but a smaller number may adjourn from day to day, and may be authorized to compel the attendance of absent members	1	5	1
It may determine the rules of its proceedings, punish a member for disorderly behavior, and with the concurrence of two-thirds expel a member	1	5	2
It shall keep a journal of its proceedings and from time to time publish the same, except such parts as may in their judgment require secrecy	1	5	3
It shall not adjourn for more than three days during a session without the consent of the other House	1	5	4
It may propose amendments to bills for raising revenue, but such bills shall originate in the House of Representatives	1	7	1
The Senate shall advise and consent to the ratification of all treaties, provided two-thirds of the members present concur	2	2	2
It shall advise and consent to the appointment of ambassadors, other public ministers and consuls, judges of the Supreme Court, and all other officers not herein otherwise provided for	2	2	2
It may be convened by the President on extraordinary occasions	2	3	1
No State, without its consent, shall be deprived of its equal suffrage in the Senate	5	....	....
Senators. They shall, immediately after assembling, under their first election, be divided into three classes, so that the seats of one-third shall become vacant at the expiration of every second year	1	3	2
No person shall be a Senator who shall not be thirty years of age, nine years a citizen of the United States, and an inhabitant when elected of the State for which he shall be chosen	1	3	3

INDEX TO THE CONSTITUTION AND AMENDMENTS—Continued

	Article [1]	Section	Clause
The times, places, and manner of choosing Senators may be fixed by the legislature of a State, but Congress may by law make or alter such regulations, except as the places of choosing	1	4	1
If vacancies happen during the recess of the legislature of a State, the executive thereof may make temporary appointments until the next meeting of the legislature	1	3	2
If vacancies happen the executive authority of the State shall issue writs of election to fill such vacancies; provided, that the legislature of any State may empower the executive thereof to make temporary appointment until the people fill the vacancies by election as the legislature may direct. [Amendments]	17	2	....
They shall in all cases, except treason, felony, and breach of the peace, be privileged from arrest during their attendance at the session of the Senate and in going to and returning from the same	1	6	1
Senators and Representatives shall receive a compensation to be ascertained by law	1	6	1
Senators and Representatives shall not be questioned for any speech or debate in either House in any other place	1	6	1
No Senator or Representative shall, during the time for which he was elected, be appointed to any civil office under the United States which shall have been created, or of which the emoluments shall have been increased during such term	1	6	2
No person holding any office under the United States shall be a member of either House during his continuance in office	1	6	2
No Senator or Representative or person holding an office of trust or profit under the United States shall be an elector for President and Vice President	2	1	2
Senators and Representatives shall be bound by an oath or affirmation to support the Constitution	6	....	3
No person shall be a Senator or Representative who, having, as a Federal or State officer, taken an oath to support the Constitution, afterward engaged in rebellion against the United States. [Amendments]	14	3	....
But Congress may, by a vote of two-thirds of each House, remove such disability. [Amendments]	14	3	....
No law, varying the compensation for the services of the Senators and Representatives, shall take effect, until an election of Representatives shall have intervened. [Amendments]	27	....	....
Service or labor in one State, escaping into another State, shall be delivered up to the party to whom such service or labor may be due. Fugitives from	4	2	3
Servitude, except as a punishment for crime, whereof the party shall have been duly convicted, shall exist in the United States or any place subject to their jurisdiction. Neither slavery nor involuntary. [Amendments]	13	1	....
Servitude. The right of citizens of the United States to vote shall not be denied or abridged by the United States or by any State, on account of race, color, or previous condition of. [Amendments]	15	1	....
Sex. Right of citizens to vote shall not be denied or abridged by the United States or any State on account of. [Amendments]	19	....	....

INDEX TO THE CONSTITUTION AND AMENDMENTS—Continued

	Article [1]	Section	Clause
Ships of war in time of peace, without the consent of Congress. No State shall keep troops or	1	10	3
Silver coin a tender in payment of debts. No State shall make anything but gold and	1	10	1
Slave. Neither the United States nor any State shall assume or pay any debt or obligation incurred in aid of insurrection or rebellion, or any claim for the loss or emancipation of any. [Amendments]	14	4	....
Slavery nor involuntary servitude, except as a punishment for crime, whereof the party shall have been duly convicted, shall exist in the United States, or any places subject to their jurisdiction. Neither. [Amendments]	13	1	....
Soldiers shall not be quartered, in time of peace, in any house without the consent of the owner. [Amendments]	3	....	....
South Carolina entitled to five Representatives in the first Congress	1	2	3
Speaker and other officers. The House of Representatives shall choose their	1	2	5
Speaker of the House of Representatives. President to transmit his declaration of inability to discharge the powers and duties of his office to. [Amendments]	25	3	....
Vice President and a majority of the principal officers of the executive departments to transmit their declaration of the President's inability to discharge the powers and duties of his office to. [Amendments]	25	4	....
Speech or of the press. Congress shall make no law abridging the freedom of. [Amendments]	1	....	....
Speedy and public trial by a jury. In all criminal prosecutions the accused shall have a. [Amendments]	6	....	....
Standard of weights and measures. Congress shall fix the	1	8	5
State legislatures, and all executive and judicial officers of the United States, shall take an oath to support the Constitution. All members of the several	6	....	3
State of the Union. The President shall, from time to time, give Congress information of the	2	3	....
States. When vacancies happen in the representation from any State, the executive authority shall issue writs of election to fill such vacancies	1	2	4
When vacancies happen in the representation of any State in the Senate, the executive authority shall issue writs of election to fill such vacancies. [Amendments]	17	2	....
Congress shall have power to regulate commerce among the several	1	8	3
No State shall enter into any treaty, alliance, or confederation	1	10	1
Shall not grant letters of marque and reprisal	1	10	1
Shall not coin money	1	10	1
Shall not emit bills of credit	1	10	1
Shall not make anything but gold and silver coin a tender in payment of debts	1	10	1
Shall not pass any bill of attainder, *ex post facto* law, or law impairing the obligation of contracts	1	10	1
Shall not grant any title of nobility	1	10	1
Shall not, without the consent of Congress, lay any duties on imports or exports, except what may be absolutely necessary for executing its inspection laws	1	10	2

INDEX TO THE CONSTITUTION AND AMENDMENTS—Continued

	Article [1]	Section	Clause
Shall not, without the consent of Congress, lay any duty of tonnage, keep troops or ships of war in time of peace, enter into any agreement or compact with another State or with a foreign power, or engage in war unless actually invaded or in such imminent danger as will not admit of delay	1	10	3
Full faith and credit in every other State shall be given to the public acts, records, and judicial proceedings of each State	4	1	....
Congress shall prescribe the manner of providing such acts, records, and proceedings	4	1	....
Citizens of each State shall be entitled to all privileges and immunities of citizens in the several States	4	2	1
New States may be admitted by Congress into this Union	4	3	1
But no new State shall be formed or erected within the jurisdiction of another State	4	3	1
Nor any State formed by the junction of two or more States or parts of States, without the consent of the legislatures as well as of Congress	4	3	1
No State shall be deprived, without its consent, of its equal suffrage in the Senate	5	....	....
Three-fourths of the legislatures of the States, or conventions of three-fourths of the States, as Congress shall prescribe, may ratify amendments to the Constitution	5	....	....
The United States shall guarantee a republican form of government to every State in the Union	4	4	....
They shall protect each State against invasion	4	4	....
And on application of the legislature, or the executive (when the legislature cannot be convened), against domestic violence	4	4	....
The ratification by nine States shall be sufficient to establish the Constitution between the States so ratifying the same	7	....	....
When the choice of President shall devolve on the House of Representatives, the vote shall be taken by States. [Amendments]	12	....	....
But in choosing the President the vote shall be taken by States, the representation from each State having one vote. [Amendments]	12	....	....
A quorum for choice of President shall consist of a member or members from two-thirds of the States, and a majority of all the States shall be necessary to a choice. [Amendments]	12	....	....
States or the people. Powers not delegated to the United States, nor prohibited to the States, are reserved to the. [Amendments]	10	....	....
Succession to the offices of the President and Vice President. [Amendments]	25	....	....
Suffrage in the Senate. No State shall be deprived without its consent of its equal	5	....	....
No denial of right to vote on account of sex. [Amendments]	19	....	....
Suits at common law, where the value in controversy shall exceed $20, shall be tried by jury. [Amendments]	7	....	....
In law or equity against one of the States, by citizens of another State, or by citizens of a foreign State. The judicial power of the United States shall not extend to. [Amendments]	11	....	....
Suppress insurrections and repel invasions. Congress shall provide for calling forth the militia to execute the laws ...	1	8	15

INDEX TO THE CONSTITUTION AND AMENDMENTS—Continued

	Article [1]	Section	Clause
Suppression of insurrection or rebellion shall not be questioned. The public debt, including the debt for pensions and bounties, incurred in the. [Amendments]	14	4	....
Supreme Court. Congress shall have power to constitute tribunals inferior to the	1	8	9
And such inferior courts as Congress may establish. The judicial power of the United States shall be vested in one	3	1	....
The judges of the Supreme Court and inferior courts shall hold their offices during good behavior	3	1	....
The compensation of the judges shall not be diminished during their continuance in office	3	1	....
Shall have original jurisdiction. In all cases affecting ambassadors, other public ministers and consuls, and in which a State may be a party, the	3	2	2
Shall have appellate jurisdiction, both as to law and the fact, with such exceptions and regulations as Congress may make. The	3	2	2
Supreme law of the land. This Constitution, the laws made in pursuance thereof, and the treaties of the United States, shall be the	6	....	2
The judges in every State shall be bound thereby	6	....	2
T			
Tax shall be laid unless in proportion to the census or enumeration. No capitation or other direct	1	9	4
Tax on incomes authorized without apportionment among the several States, and without regard to any census or enumeration. [Amendments]	16	....	....
Tax or duty shall be laid on articles exported from any State. No	1	9	5
Tax. The right of citizens of the United States to vote shall not be denied or abridged by the United States or any State by reason of failure to pay. [Amendments]	24	1	....
Taxes (direct) and Representatives, how apportioned among the several States	1	2	3
Taxes, duties, imposts, and excises. Congress shall have power to lay	1	8	1
They shall be uniform throughout the United States	1	8	1
Temporary appointments until the next meeting of the legislature. If vacancies happen in the Senate in the recess of the legislature of a State, the executive of the State shall make	1	3	2
Tender in payment of debts. No State shall make anything but gold and silver coin a	1	10	1
Term for which he is elected. No Senator or Representative shall be appointed to any office under the United States which shall have been created or its emoluments increased during the	1	6	2
Term of office. President, not more than twice. [Amendments]	22	....	....
Terms of four years. The President and Vice President shall hold their offices for the	2	1	1
Territory or other property of the United States. Congress shall dispose of and make all needful rules and regulations respecting the	4	3	2
Test as a qualification for any office or public trust shall ever be required. No religious	6	....	3
Testimony of two witnesses to the same overt act, or on confession in open court. No person shall be convicted of treason except on the	3	3	1

INDEX TO THE CONSTITUTION AND AMENDMENTS—Continued

	Article [1]	Section	Clause
Three-fourths of the legislatures of the States, or conventions in three-fourths of the States, as Congress shall prescribe, may ratify amendments to the Constitution	5	....	....
Tie. The Vice President shall have no vote unless the Senate be equally divided	1	3	4
Times, places, and manner of holding elections for Senators and Representatives shall be prescribed in each State by the legislature thereof	1	4	1
But Congress may at any time by law make or alter such regulations, except as to the places of choosing Senators	1	4	1
Title of any kind, from any king, prince, or foreign State, without the consent of Congress. No person holding any office under the United States shall accept of any	1	9	8
Title of nobility. The United States shall not grant any	1	9	8
No State shall grant any	1	10	1
Tonnage without the consent of Congress. No State shall lay any duty of	1	10	3
Tranquility, provide for the common defense, &c. To insure domestic. [Preamble]	....	....	....
Treason shall consist only in levying war against the United States, or in adhering to their enemies, giving them aid and comfort	3	3	1
No person shall, unless on the testimony of two witnesses to the same overt act, or on confession in open court, be convicted of	3	3	1
Congress shall have power to declare the punishment of	3	3	2
Shall not work corruption of blood. Attainder of	3	3	2
Shall not work forfeiture, except during the life of the person attainted. Attainder of	3	3	2
Treason, bribery, or other high crimes and misdemeanors. The President, Vice President, and all civil officers shall be removed from office on impeachment for and conviction of	2	4	1
Treason, felony, and breach of the peace. Senators and Representatives shall be privileged from arrest while attending or while going to or returning from the sessions of Congress, except in cases of	1	6	1
Treasury, but in consequence of appropriations made by law. No money shall be drawn from the	1	9	7
Treaties. The President shall have power, with the advice and consent of the Senate, provided two-thirds of the Senators present concur, to make	2	2	2
The judicial power shall extend to all cases arising under the Constitution, laws, and	3	2	1
They shall be the supreme law of the land, and the judges in every State shall be bound thereby	6	....	2
Treaty, alliance, or confederation. No State shall enter into any	1	10	1
Trial, judgment, and punishment according to law. Judgment in cases of impeachment shall not extend further than to removal from, and disqualification for, office; but the party convicted shall nevertheless be liable and subject to indictment	1	3	7
Trial by jury. All crimes, except in cases of impeachment, shall be tried by jury	3	2	3
Such trial shall be held in the State within which the crime shall have been committed	3	2	3
But when not committed within a State, the trial shall be at such a place as Congress may by law have directed	3	2	3

INDEX TO THE CONSTITUTION AND AMENDMENTS—Continued

	Article [1]	Section	Clause
In all criminal prosecutions the accused shall have a speedy and public. [Amendments]	6	....	....
Suits at common law, when the amount exceeds $20, shall be by. [Amendments]	7	....	....
Tribunals, inferior to the Supreme Court. Congress shall have power to constitute	1	8	9
Troops or ships of war in time of peace without the consent of Congress. No State shall keep	1	10	3
Trust or profit under the United States, shall be an elector for President and Vice President. No Senator, Representative, or person holding any office of	2	1	2
Two-thirds of the members present. No person shall be convicted on an impeachment without the concurrence of	1	3	6
Two-thirds, may expel a member. Each House, with the concurrence of	1	5	2
Two-thirds. A bill returned by the President with his objections, may be repassed by each House by a vote of	1	7	2
Two-thirds of the Senators present concur. The President shall have power, by and with the advice and consent of the Senate, to make treaties, provided	2	2	2
Two-thirds of the legislatures of the several States. Congress shall call a convention for proposing amendments to the Constitution on the application of	5	....	....
Two-thirds of both Houses shall deem it necessary. Congress shall propose amendments to the Constitution whenever	5	....	....
Two-thirds of the States. When the choice of a President shall devolve on the House of Representatives, a quorum shall consist of a member or members from. [Amendments]	12	....	....
Two-thirds of the whole number of Senators. A quorum of the Senate, when choosing a Vice President, shall consist of. [Amendments]	12	....	....
Two-thirds may remove the disabilities imposed by the third section of the fourteenth amendment. Congress, by a vote of. [Amendments]	14	3	....
Two years. Appropriations for raising and supporting armies shall not be for a longer term than	1	8	12
U			
Union. To establish a more perfect. [Preamble]	....	....	....
The President shall, from time to time, give to Congress information of the state of the	2	3	1
New States may be admitted by Congress into this	4	3	1
But no new States shall be formed or erected within the jurisdiction of another	4	3	1
Unreasonable searches and seizures. The people shall be secured in their persons, houses, papers, and effects against. [Amendments]	4	....	....
And no warrants shall be issued but upon probable cause, supported by oath or affirmation, and particularly describing the place to be searched, and the persons or things to be seized. [Amendments]	4	....	....
Unusual punishments inflicted. Excessive bail shall not be required, nor excessive fines imposed, nor cruel and. [Amendments]	8	....	....
Use without just compensation. Private property shall not be taken for public. [Amendments]	5	....	....

INDEX TO THE CONSTITUTION AND AMENDMENTS—Continued

	Article [1]	Section	Clause
Useful arts, by securing for limited times to authors and inventors the exclusive right to their writings and inventions. Congress shall have power to promote the progress of science and the	1	8	8
V			
Vacancies happening in the representation of a State. The executive thereof shall issue writs of election to fill	1	2	4
Vacancies happening in the representation of a State in the Senate. The executive thereof shall issue writs of election to fill. [Amendments]	17	2	....
Vacancies happening in the Senate in the recess of the legislature of a State. How filled	1	3	2
Vacancies that happen during the recess of the Senate, by granting commissions which shall expire at the end of the next session. The President shall have power to fill	2	2	3
Validity of the public debt incurred in suppressing insurrection against the United States, including debt for pensions and bounties, shall not be questioned. [Amendments]	14	4	....
Vessels bound to or from the ports of one State, shall not be obliged to enter, clear, or pay duties in another State	1	9	6
Veto of a bill by the President. Proceedings of the two Houses upon the	1	7	2
Vice President of the United States shall be President of the Senate	1	3	4
He shall have no vote unless the Senate be equally divided	1	3	4
The Senate shall choose a President *pro tempore* in the absence of the	1	3	5
He shall be chosen for the term of four years	2	1	1
The number and the manner of appointing electors for President and	2	1	2
In case of the removal, death, resignation, or inability of the President, the powers and duties of his office shall devolve on the	2	1	6
[Amendments]	25	....	....
Congress may provide by law for the case of the removal, death, resignation, or inability both of the President and	2	1	6
[Amendments]	25	....	....
On impeachment for and conviction of treason, bribery, and other high crimes and misdemeanors, shall be removed from office. The	2	4	....
Vice President. The manner of choosing the. The electors shall meet in their respective States and vote by ballot for President and Vice President, one of whom, at least, shall not be an inhabitant of the same State with themselves. [Amendments]	12	....	....
Additionial provision for succession through act of Congress. [Amendments]	20	4	....
Nomination by President in case of vacancy in office. [Amendments]	25	2	....
Term of office, beginning and ending. [Amendments]	20	1	....
The electors shall name, in distinct ballots, the person voted for as Vice President. [Amendments]	12	....	....
They shall make distinct lists of the persons voted for as Vice President, which lists they shall sign and certify, and send sealed to the seat of Government, directed to the President of the Senate. [Amendments]	12	....	....

INDEX TO THE CONSTITUTION AND AMENDMENTS—Continued

	Article[1]	Section	Clause
The President of the Senate shall, in the presence of the Senate and House of Representatives, open all the certificates, and the votes shall be then counted. [Amendments]	12	....	....
The person having the greatest number of votes shall be Vice President, if such number be a majority of the whole number of electors. [Amendments]	12	....	....
If no person have a majority, then from the two highest numbers on the list the Senate shall choose the Vice President. [Amendments]	12	....	....
A quorum for this purpose shall consist of two-thirds of the whole number of Senators; and a majority of the whole number shall be necessary to a choice. [Amendments]	12	....	....
But if the House shall make no choice of a President before the 4th of March next following, then the Vice President shall act as President, as in the case of the death or other constitutional disability of the President. [Amendments]	12	....	....
No person constitutionally ineligible as President shall be eligible as. [Amendments]	12	....	....
In case of the removal, death, resignation, or inability of the President, the powers and duties of his office shall succeed to. [Amendments]	25	....	....
Nomination by President of successor in event of vacancy in office of. [Amendments]	25	2	....
Violence. The United States shall guarantee to every State a republican form of government, and shall protect each State against invasion and domestic	4	4	....
Virginia entitled to ten Representatives in the first Congress	1	2	3
Vote. Each Senator shall have one	1	3	1
The Vice President, unless the Senate be equally divided, shall have no	1	3	4
Requiring the concurrence of the two Houses (except upon a question of adjournment) shall be presented to the President. Every order, resolution, or	1	7	3
Shall not be denied or abridged by the United States or by any State on account of race, color, or previous condition of servitude. The right of citizens of the United States to. [Amendments]	15	1	....
Right of citizens to vote shall not be denied or abridged by the United States or any State on account of sex. [Amendments]	19	....	....
Shall not be denied or abridged by the United States or any State by reason of failure to pay any poll tax or other tax. The right of citizens of the United States to. [Amendments]	24	1	....
Right of citizens who are eighteen years of age or older to vote shall not be denied or abridged by the United States or any State, on account of age. [Amendments]	26	1	....
Vote of two-thirds. Each House may expel a member by a ..	1	5	2
A bill vetoed by the President may be repassed in each House by a	1	7	2
No person shall be convicted on an impeachment except by a	1	3	6
Whenever both Houses shall deem it necessary, Congress may propose amendments to the Constitution by a	5	....	....

INDEX TO THE CONSTITUTION AND AMENDMENTS—Continued

	Article [1]	Section	Clause
The President may make treaties with the advice and consent of the Senate, by a	2	2	2
Disabilities incurred by participation in insurrection or rebellion, may be relieved by Congress by a. [Amendments]	14	3	....
W			
War, grant letters of marque and reprisal, and make rules concerning captures on land and water. Congress shall have power to declare	1	8	11
For governing the land and naval forces. Congress shall have power to make rules and articles of	1	8	14
No State shall, without the consent of Congress, unless actually invaded, or in such imminent danger as will not admit of delay, engage in	1	10	3
War against the United States, adhering to their enemies, and giving them aid and comfort. Treason shall consist only in levying	3	3	1
Warrants shall issue but upon probable cause, on oath or affirmation, describing the place to be searched, and the person or things to be seized. No. [Amendments]	4	....	....
Weights and measures. Congress shall fix the standard of	1	8	5
Welfare and to secure the blessings of liberty, &c. To promote the general. [Preamble]	....	....	....
Welfare. Congress shall have power to provide for the common defense and general	1	8	1
Witness against himself. No person shall, in a criminal case, be compelled to be a. [Amendments]	5	....	....
Witnesses against him. In all criminal prosecutions the accused shall be confronted with the. [Amendments]	6	....	....
Witnesses in his favor. In all criminal prosecutions the accused shall have compulsory process for obtaining. [Amendments]	6	....	....
Witnesses to the same overt act, or on confession in open court. No person shall be convicted of treason unless on the testimony of two	3	3	1
Writ of habeas corpus shall not be suspended unless in case of rebellion or invasion the public safety may require it	1	9	2
Writs of election to fill vacancies in the representation of any State. The executives of the State shall issue	1	2	4
Written opinion of the principal officer in each of the Executive Departments on any subject relating to the duties of his office. The President may require the	2	2	1
Y			
Yeas and nays of the members of either House shall, at the desire of one-fifth of those present, be entered on the journals	1	5	3
The votes of both Houses upon the reconsideration of a bill returned by the President with his objections shall be determined by	1	7	2

○